Blender Unleashed: Mastering the Art of 3D Creation

Kameron Hussain and Frahaan Hussain

Published by Sonar Publishing, 2023.

BLENDER UNLEASHED: MASTERING THE ART OF 3D CREATION

First edition. December 13, 2023.

ISBN: 979-8215623916

Written by Kameron Hussain and Frahaan Hussain.

Table of Contents

10.4: Staying Updated with Industry Trends and Blender Updates

1. Follow Industry News:

2. Social Media Engagement:

3. Online Courses and Tutorials:

4. Conferences and Events:

5. Blender Foundation's Official Channels:

6. User Communities:

7. Experiment and Explore:

8. Networking with Peers:

9. Feedback and Critique:

10. Blender Documentation:

11. Community Projects:

12. Professional Development:

13. Feedback Loop with Blender Developers:

10.5: Future Directions and Emerging Technologies in 3D Graphics

1. Real-Time Rendering:

2. Virtual Reality (VR) and Augmented Reality (AR):

3. AI and Machine Learning:

4. Realistic Physics and Simulations:

1. Virtual Reality (VR) and Augmented Reality (AR)
2. Architectural Visualization
3. Game Development
4. Medical Visualization and Simulation
5. Education and Training
6. Film and Animation
7. Product Design and Visualization
8. Scientific Visualization
9. Art and Entertainment

20.4 Educating the Next Generation of Blender Artists

1. Incorporating Blender into Curricula
2. Online Learning Resources
3. Blender Foundation's Education Program
4. Open Source and Cost-Effective
5. Industry-Relevant Skills
6. Artistic Expression and Creativity
7. Career Opportunities
8. Blender Competitions and Challenges

20.5 Envisioning the Future of Blender and 3D Artistry

1. Realism and Immersion

2. AI-Powered Creativity

3. Accessibility and Inclusivity

4. Collaboration and Community

5. Blender for Emerging Technologies

6. Cross-Platform Integration

7. Blender's Role in Education

8. Environmental and Sustainability Initiatives

9. Artistic Freedom and Innovation

Chapter 1: Entering the Blender Universe

1.1 Introduction to Blender 3D: History and Evolution

Blender, an open-source 3D graphics and animation software, has a rich history that dates back to the early 1990s. Initially developed by Ton Roosendaal in the Netherlands, Blender began as an in-house tool for a small animation studio. The early versions focused on providing a compact, yet powerful suite for 3D modeling and animation.

In the late 1990s, Blender's potential grew, but the studio faced financial challenges. This led to a pivotal moment in Blender's history - the decision to release it as an open-source software in 2002. The Blender community, passionate about the tool, rallied to raise funds, ensuring Blender's development continued.

As an open-source project, Blender saw rapid evolution, with contributions from programmers worldwide. Each version brought significant improvements, making it more user-friendly and powerful. For instance, the introduction of the Cycles rendering engine in the 2010s marked a leap in rendering capabilities, allowing artists to create photorealistic images.

Blender's interface has also evolved. Initially criticized for its steep learning curve, recent versions have become more intuitive, attracting a broader user base. The 2.8 update, in particular, was a major overhaul, introducing a more streamlined and modern interface.

One of Blender's strengths lies in its versatility. It's not just a 3D modeling tool; it's equipped for the entire 3D pipeline. This includes sculpting, rigging, animation, simulation, rendering, compositing, and motion tracking. This versatility makes it a popular choice for indie developers, small studios, and hobbyists.

Blender also integrates well with other software. It supports various file formats, allowing for seamless integration into various workflows. This adaptability extends to its scripting capabilities, with Python as its scripting language. This allows for customization and automation, a feature that advanced users greatly appreciate.

```
# Example of a simple Python script in Blender

import bpy

# Create a new mesh (a simple cube)

mesh = bpy.data.meshes.new(name='MyCube')

obj = bpy.data.objects.new(name='MyCube', object_data=mesh)

# Link it to the scene

bpy.context.collection.objects.link(obj)

# Generate the geometry (a simple cube)

verts = [(1, 1, -1), (1, -1, -1), (-1, -1, -1), (-1, 1, -1), (1, 1, 1), (1, -1, 1), (-1, -1, 1), (-1, 1, 1)]

edges = []

faces = [(0, 1, 2, 3), (4, 7, 6, 5), (0, 4, 5, 1), (1, 5, 6, 2), (2, 6, 7, 3), (4, 0, 3, 7)]

mesh.from_pydata(verts, edges, faces)
```

```
mesh.update()
```

The Blender community plays a crucial role in its development. The community not only contributes code but also creates tutorials, shares resources, and offers support to fellow users. This collaborative environment fosters learning and innovation.

Blender's impact on the industry is significant, particularly in the realms of indie game development, small-scale film production, and visual effects. It's been used in various notable projects, showcasing its capability to compete with high-end, commercial 3D software.

The Blender Foundation, established to support Blender's development, organizes conferences and participates in various industry events. This helps in gathering feedback, understanding user needs, and aligning development goals with the community's needs.

Looking at Blender's evolution, it's clear that it has grown from a niche tool to a major player in the 3D graphics industry. Its future seems bright, with continuous updates and an ever-growing community of users and developers.

In conclusion, Blender 3D's journey from a small in-house tool to a leading open-source 3D graphics software is a testament to the power of community-driven development. Its comprehensive toolset, open-source nature, and strong community support make it an invaluable asset for anyone interested in 3D graphics, animation, and digital art.

1.2 Navigating the Blender Interface: A Guided Tour

Navigating Blender's interface is crucial for efficiently using the software. The interface, known for its complexity, can be daunting for beginners. However, understanding its layout and functionality is key to mastering Blender.

When you first open Blender, you're greeted with the default screen layout. This layout is divided into several areas: the 3D viewport, timeline, outliner, and properties panel. Each area serves a specific purpose in the 3D creation process.

The 3D viewport is the heart of Blender. It's where you interact with your models, sculpt, animate, and view your scenes. You can navigate the viewport using mouse controls: the middle mouse button to orbit, scroll wheel to zoom, and shift + middle mouse button to pan.

Blender uses a unique system of "editors" for different tasks. For instance, the 3D viewport is one editor, the timeline is another, and so is the properties panel. You can change any of these areas to a different editor based on your needs.

The timeline at the bottom is essential for animation. It displays the current frame and allows you to scrub through your animation. Keyframes can be added and modified here for animating objects.

The outliner, usually found on the top right, is like a table of contents for your scene. It lists all objects, cameras, lights, and other elements in your scene. You can select, hide, or lock elements from here.

The properties panel, adjacent to the outliner, is where you adjust the details of your selected object. This includes object properties, modifiers, materials, and render settings. Each set of properties is organized into tabs for easy navigation.

Customizing your workspace in Blender is straightforward. You can drag the edges of any area to resize it. If you want more space for a specific editor, you can even join two areas into one.

For those who prefer using keyboard shortcuts, Blender offers a wide range. For example, 'G' is used for grab/move, 'R' for rotate, and 'S' for scale. Learning these shortcuts can significantly speed up your workflow.

Blender's interface also supports multiple views and layouts. You can have different layouts for modeling, sculpting, UV editing, etc. Switching between these layouts can be done with a few clicks, optimizing your workspace for the task at hand.

The power of Blender's interface lies in its customization. You can add or remove buttons, change themes, and even create your own menus. This level of customization ensures that you can create a workspace that perfectly fits your workflow.

```
# Example of a simple Python script to customize the Blender interface

import bpy

# Define a new panel class

class MyCustomPanel(bpy.types.Panel):

bl_label = "My Custom Panel"

bl_idname = "OBJECT_PT_my_custom_panel"

bl_space_type = 'VIEW_3D'

bl_region_type = 'UI'

bl_category = 'Tools'
```

```
def draw(self, context):
layout = self.layout
layout.label(text="This is a custom panel")
# Register the panel class
def register():
bpy.utils.register_class(MyCustomPanel)
def unregister():
bpy.utils.unregister_class(MyCustomPanel)
if __name__ == "__main__":
register()
```

Blender's interface also includes a powerful node editor. This is used for creating complex materials, textures, and even compositing effects in a non-linear, visual way.

The file browser, another crucial part of the interface, is not just for opening and saving files. It can also be used to import assets, link or append objects from other Blender files, and manage your project's external data.

Blender's interface can be overwhelming at first, but it's designed to be efficient for a wide range of 3D tasks. Spending time learning and customizing it to fit your workflow is a worthwhile investment.

In summary, Blender's interface is a complex but highly customizable environment. Understanding its layout, editors, and functionality is essential for anyone looking to create 3D content. With practice and customization, it becomes a powerful tool in your 3D creation arsenal.

1.3 Understanding Blender's Core Concepts and Workflow

Blender's workflow and core concepts are foundational to mastering this powerful 3D software. It integrates various aspects of 3D creation, from modeling and texturing to animation and rendering, each with its unique workflow and set of tools.

At the heart of Blender's workflow is the concept of a scene. A scene in Blender is a container for all your objects, lights, cameras, and other elements. Understanding how to manage and organize scenes is crucial for any project.

Objects are the building blocks of any Blender scene. They can be anything from simple shapes like cubes and spheres to complex models imported from other software. In Blender, you manipulate objects using operations like move, rotate, and scale.

Modeling is the first step in most 3D projects. Blender offers a range of modeling tools, from basic extrusion and beveling to advanced sculpting tools. Understanding the principles of topology and geometry is essential for creating clean, efficient models.

Texturing and materials add realism to your models. In Blender, you can create detailed textures and apply various materials to give your objects color, shininess, transparency, and more. The node-based material editor allows for complex and realistic material creation.

Lighting in Blender is another vital concept. Proper lighting can bring a scene to life, highlighting details and setting the mood.

Blender offers several types of lights, each with its own set of properties and uses.

Camera placement and animation are crucial for visualizing your scene. In Blender, you can position and animate cameras to capture your scene from different angles and perspectives. Understanding camera settings like focal length and depth of field is important for creating compelling visuals.

Animation is a powerful feature in Blender. It involves bringing objects to life, whether it's simple motion or complex character animations. Blender supports keyframe animation, shape keys, and armatures for character rigging.

Rendering is the process of turning your 3D scene into a final image or animation. Blender offers two main rendering engines: Cycles and Eevee. Each has its strengths and ideal use cases, from photorealistic renders to fast, real-time previews.

Post-processing and compositing are the final steps in the Blender workflow. They involve refining your rendered images or footage, adding effects, or combining them with other elements. Blender's compositor offers a range of tools for post-processing.

Blender also supports simulations and physics. You can create realistic motion and effects with tools for fluid, cloth, smoke, and rigid body dynamics. These tools can add a lot of realism and dynamism to your scenes.

Blender's Python API opens up possibilities for automation and custom tool creation. With Python scripting, you can automate repetitive tasks, create custom operators, or even develop new add-ons to extend Blender's functionality.

 # Example Python script to create a simple animation in Blender

```
import bpy

# Select the default cube

cube = bpy.data.objects['Cube']

# Set the start and end frames for the animation

bpy.context.scene.frame_start = 1

bpy.context.scene.frame_end = 60

# Insert keyframes for the cube's location

cube.location.x = 0

cube.keyframe_insert(data_path="location", frame=1)

cube.location.x = 10

cube.keyframe_insert(data_path="location", frame=60)
```

Blender's workflow is non-linear, meaning you can move between different stages like modeling, texturing, and rendering seamlessly. This flexibility allows artists to iterate and refine their work efficiently.

Collaboration and project management are also important in Blender. The software supports linking and appending objects from other files, making it easier to collaborate on larger projects.

Understanding Blender's core concepts and workflow is essential for anyone looking to create professional-quality 3D content. While it has a steep learning curve, the breadth and depth of Blender's capabilities make it a powerful tool in the hands of a skilled artist.

1.4 Setting Up Your First Project in Blender

Setting up your first project in Blender is an exciting step towards creating 3D art. It involves several key steps, from understanding the initial settings to organizing your workspace for efficient workflow.

When you first open Blender, you're presented with a default scene. This scene typically includes a camera, a light, and a cube. Understanding these elements is crucial as they form the basis of any project.

Before you start modeling, it's important to set up your scene. This includes choosing the right units for your project (metric or imperial), setting up the grid scale, and adjusting the world settings for appropriate background colors or environment textures.

Organizing your workspace is essential for efficiency. Blender's flexible interface allows you to customize the layout to suit your needs. You can create separate layouts for modeling, texturing, animating, and more.

Choosing the right renderer is another important decision. Blender offers two main render engines: Cycles and Eevee. Cycles is a ray-trace based renderer known for its photorealism, while Eevee is a real-time renderer offering faster results. Your choice depends on your project's needs and the power of your hardware.

Creating and saving a user template can save time for future projects. Once you have a workspace layout that suits your workflow, you can save it as a template and start with this layout every time you open Blender.

Understanding and setting up the camera is crucial for framing your scenes. You can adjust the focal length, depth of field, and other settings to achieve the desired perspective and composition.

The next step is to start creating your objects. In Blender, you can either start with basic shapes (like cubes, spheres, etc.) and modify them, or you can import models from other sources.

When modeling, it's important to keep an eye on the topology of your meshes, especially if you plan to animate them. Good topology ensures smooth deformations during animation and can improve render times.

Materials and texturing bring life to your models. Blender's material system is highly versatile, allowing for the creation of a wide range of materials. You can use both procedural textures (generated within Blender) and image textures (imported from external sources).

Lighting is crucial in defining the mood and realism of your scene. Experiment with different light types and settings to find the best look for your project. Blender's light objects, such as point, sun, and spotlights, offer various options to control the light's intensity, color, and direction.

Animation is a key part of many Blender projects. If your project involves animation, setting up keyframes and understanding the basics of motion paths is important.

Rendering is the final step in visualizing your project. It's important to understand render settings like resolution, sampling, and output format to get the best quality and efficiency.

Post-processing in Blender can enhance your rendered images. Using the compositor, you can add effects like blur, color correction, and glare to your final render.

Managing your project files and assets is crucial, especially for larger projects. Organizing your files into a logical structure and naming them appropriately will save you time and frustration in the long run.

Backing up your work regularly is important. Blender projects can become quite complex, and losing progress due to a crash or mistake can be frustrating.

```
# Example Python script to automate a simple task in Blender
import bpy
# Deselect all objects
bpy.ops.object.select_all(action='DESELECT')
# Select all mesh objects
for obj in bpy.data.objects:
if obj.type == 'MESH':
obj.select_set(True)
```

In summary, setting up your first project in Blender involves understanding the interface, customizing your workspace, setting up the scene, creating models, applying materials and textures, setting up lighting and cameras, and finally rendering your scene. Each step is important and contributes to the successful completion of your project.

1.5 Exploring the Community and Resources for Blender Users

The Blender community is a vibrant and supportive ecosystem, offering a wealth of resources for users of all skill levels. Engaging with this community can greatly enhance your Blender experience, providing access to tutorials, forums, and collaborative opportunities.

One of the first places new Blender users should explore is the official Blender website. It hosts a variety of resources, including tutorials, documentation, and links to download the latest version of Blender. The site also features case studies and news about the latest developments in the software.

Online forums and social media groups are invaluable for getting help, sharing work, and networking with other Blender users. Platforms like Blender Artists Forum, Reddit's r/blender, and Blender Stack Exchange are popular among the Blender community. These forums are a great place to ask questions, get feedback on your work, and stay updated with Blender news.

Blender tutorials are available in abundance online, catering to all skill levels. Websites like Blender Guru, CG Cookie, and YouTube host a plethora of tutorials covering basic to advanced topics. These tutorials are invaluable for self-learning and improving your skills.

Participating in Blender challenges and competitions is a great way to improve your skills and get noticed in the community. These events, often hosted on forums or social media, encourage creativity and offer a fun way to engage with other users.

Blender's extensive documentation is an essential resource. It includes detailed information on every aspect of the software, from basic navigation to advanced features. The Blender Manual is regularly updated with each new version of Blender, ensuring the information is current.

Blender conferences and meetups are events where users can connect in person. These events often feature workshops, presentations, and networking opportunities. The Blender Conference, held annually in Amsterdam, is one of the most notable events in the Blender community.

Blender add-ons can greatly enhance the software's functionality. The Blender Market and Gumroad are popular platforms for finding both free and paid add-ons. These add-ons can range from workflow enhancements to new modeling tools.

Open-source projects and collaborative efforts are a core part of the Blender community. Participating in these projects can provide valuable experience and help you connect with other Blender enthusiasts.

The Blender Network is a professional network for Blender users. It's a platform for finding and offering Blender-related services, connecting freelance artists, studios, and educators with clients.

Blender Cloud is another resource offering training, assets, and project management tools. It's a subscription-based service provided by the Blender Foundation, supporting the development of Blender.

YouTube is a treasure trove for Blender learning materials. Many experienced Blender artists share their knowledge through video tutorials, covering a wide range of topics from beginner guides to advanced techniques.

Books and e-books are also valuable resources for learning Blender. These often provide a structured approach to learning and cover topics in greater depth than many online tutorials.

Podcasts and blogs about Blender offer insights into the software and the community. Listening to experiences and tips from seasoned Blender artists can be both educational and inspiring.

Artwork galleries, such as those on ArtStation and Behance, showcase Blender projects. These galleries can provide inspiration and an understanding of what's possible with the software.

Collaborative projects, like open movies and games produced by the Blender Foundation, demonstrate the capabilities of Blender in a professional production environment. These projects also provide learning materials and assets for the community.

Blender's API allows for scripting and customization. Users with programming knowledge can automate tasks, create custom tools, and even contribute to Blender's development.

```
# Example Python script to create a custom operator in Blender

import bpy

class SimpleOperator(bpy.types.Operator):

"""Tooltip"""

bl_idname = "object.simple_operator"

bl_label = "Simple Object Operator"

def execute(self, context):

context.object.location.x += 1.0

return {'FINISHED'}

def register():

bpy.utils.register_class(SimpleOperator)

def unregister():

bpy.utils.unregister_class(SimpleOperator)

if __name__ == "__main__":

register()
```

In conclusion, the Blender community is a rich and diverse source of knowledge, inspiration, and collaboration. By engaging with these resources, you can significantly enhance your Blender skills and enjoy a more rewarding 3D creation experience.

Chapter 2: Modeling Magic

2.1 The Basics of 3D Modeling in Blender

3D modeling in Blender is a foundational skill for creating anything from simple objects to complex scenes. Understanding the basics of modeling is essential for any aspiring 3D artist.

When you begin modeling in Blender, you start with a basic shape, known as a primitive. These primitives, such as cubes, spheres, and cylinders, can be manipulated to form more complex shapes. Blender offers a variety of primitives to start your modeling projects.

The fundamental operations in 3D modeling are scaling, moving, and rotating objects. In Blender, these are easily accessible through shortcuts 'S' for scaling, 'G' for moving (grabbing), and 'R' for rotating.

Another important aspect of modeling is understanding vertices, edges, and faces. These are the building blocks of your 3D models. Vertices are points in 3D space, edges connect vertices, and faces are the flat surfaces enclosed by edges.

Editing these components is done in Edit Mode, one of Blender's most powerful features. In Edit Mode, you can extrude, bevel, loop cut, and perform various other operations to shape your model.

Extrusion is a fundamental technique in 3D modeling. It involves extending a face or edge to add more geometry to your model. This is often used to create complex shapes from simple ones.

Subdivision surface modeling is a technique used to create smooth and organic shapes. It involves subdividing the faces of the model to increase its geometry and then shaping it to the desired form.

Modifiers in Blender are tools that non-destructively alter your model. A common modifier is the Subdivision Surface modifier, which smooths the model without permanently changing its base geometry.

The importance of good topology cannot be overstated. Topology refers to the layout of vertices, edges, and faces in your model. Good topology is essential for models that deform, like characters, as it ensures smooth and predictable deformations.

Modeling for animation requires a special approach. You need to consider how the model will move and ensure that the topology supports these movements without any distortions.

UV mapping is the process of projecting a 3D model onto a 2D plane for texturing. It's an important step in preparing your model for realistic texturing.

Blender also offers sculpting tools for more organic and detailed modeling. Sculpting is akin to working with digital clay, where you can push, pull, and carve your model to add fine details.

Boolean operations are a powerful way to create complex shapes. They allow you to combine objects using union, difference, and intersection operations.

Using reference images is crucial for accurate modeling, especially when recreating real-world objects or characters. Blender allows you to import and align reference images in your 3D viewport.

Precision modeling is essential for architectural and mechanical designs. Blender offers tools for exact measurements and alignments, ensuring accuracy in your models.

The Grease Pencil tool in Blender is a unique feature that lets you draw in 3D space. It can be used for planning, annotation, or even as a base for modeling.

Retopology is the process of creating a new, optimized mesh for complex or high-polygon models. It's crucial for animation and game asset creation, ensuring efficient and smooth models.

```
# Example Python script to create a simple 3D object in Blender

import bpy

# Define the vertices and faces of the object

verts = [(0, 0, 0), (0, 2, 0), (2, 2, 0), (2, 0, 0)]

faces = [(0, 1, 2, 3)]

# Create a new mesh and object

mesh = bpy.data.meshes.new(name="MyMesh")

obj = bpy.data.objects.new(name="MyObject", object_data=mesh)

# Link the object to the scene

bpy.context.collection.objects.link(obj)

# Fill the mesh with vertices and faces

mesh.from_pydata(verts, [], faces)

mesh.update()
```

In conclusion, mastering the basics of 3D modeling in Blender opens up a world of creative possibilities. From simple shapes to intricate designs, the tools and techniques available in Blender provide a robust platform for any 3D modeling project.

2.2 Advanced Modeling Techniques: Sculpting and Texturing

Advancing from basic 3D modeling, Blender offers a suite of tools for sculpting and texturing, allowing artists to add intricate details and realistic finishes to their models. These advanced techniques can elevate a simple 3D model to a piece of art.

Sculpting in Blender is akin to working with digital clay. It allows for a more intuitive and artistic approach to shaping your models. Blender's sculpting mode offers various brushes for carving, smoothing, pulling, pushing, and inflating the digital clay.

Dynamic topology is a feature in sculpting that adds geometry dynamically as you sculpt. This means that the more detail you add, the more Blender refines the mesh locally, allowing for intricate details without overloading the entire model with vertices.

Remeshing is another technique used in conjunction with sculpting. It helps in creating a uniform topology, which is particularly useful for 3D printing or animation.

Multiresolution sculpting is a method that lets you work on different levels of detail. You can start sculpting on a low-resolution mesh and gradually add more details on higher resolutions. This approach is beneficial for maintaining a manageable workflow and for animations.

Texturing in Blender is the process of applying images or procedural patterns to give color, bump, reflection, and other properties to your model. Blender's node-based material system allows for complex and layered textures.

UV unwrapping is essential for applying image textures correctly. It involves unwrapping the 3D model into a 2D plane to allow for accurate texture placement. Blender offers various unwrapping methods, including smart projections and manual seam marking.

Procedural texturing uses mathematical functions to create textures. These textures can be infinitely detailed and don't suffer from resolution limitations like image textures. They can be mixed and manipulated to create unique materials.

Baking is a process where you transfer details from a high-poly model to a low-poly model, often used in game asset creation. This includes baking normal maps, which store detailed surface information in an image.

Displacement mapping is a technique used to add high-resolution detail to a model. Unlike normal or bump mapping, displacement mapping actually alters the geometry, resulting in more realistic details.

Vertex painting is a method to directly paint colors onto the vertices of a model. This can be used for quick texturing or as a guide for further material development.

Material nodes in Blender are used to create complex materials. They can be anything from simple colors and textures to intricate shaders simulating real-world materials like skin, metal, or glass.

The Shader Editor in Blender is a powerful tool for creating and manipulating materials. It allows you to visually connect nodes to build complex shaders.

Environmental texturing involves creating textures that respond to the environment, like reflective surfaces or materials that change appearance under different lighting conditions.

Texture painting allows you to paint textures directly onto the model. This can be done in 3D view, giving you real-time feedback on how the texture looks on the model.

Blender also supports PBR (Physically Based Rendering) materials, which provide more realistic results by simulating how light interacts with surfaces in the real world.

```
# Example Python script to change the material of an object in Blender

import bpy

# Create a new material

material = bpy.data.materials.new(name="MyMaterial")

material.use_nodes = True

nodes = material.node_tree.nodes

# Remove default nodes

for node in nodes:

nodes.remove(node)

# Add a new Principled BSDF shader node

shader = nodes.new(type='ShaderNodeBsdfPrincipled')

shader.location = (0, 0)

# Add a Material Output node

output = nodes.new(type='ShaderNodeOutputMaterial')

output.location = (200, 0)

# Link the Principled BSDF shader to Material Output
```

```
material.node_tree.links.new(shader.outputs['BSDF'], output.inputs['Surface'])

# Assign the material to the first object in the scene

bpy.context.scene.objects[0].data.materials.append(material)
```

In summary, mastering sculpting and texturing in Blender can dramatically enhance the realism and artistic quality of 3D models. These advanced techniques, while more complex, offer greater control and creativity in the 3D modeling process.

2.3 Utilizing Modifiers for Efficient Modeling

Modifiers in Blender are powerful tools that automate and simplify complex modeling tasks. They can be used non-destructively, allowing for flexibility and experimentation in the modeling process.

The Subdivision Surface Modifier is one of the most commonly used modifiers. It smooths and subdivides the mesh, making it more detailed and smooth. This is particularly useful for creating organic shapes and characters.

The Array Modifier creates copies of the original mesh in an array. This is useful for objects that need to be repeated multiple times, like tiles, stairs, or patterns. The modifier allows for adjustments in the number, distance, and orientation of the copies.

The Boolean Modifier is a tool for combining or subtracting shapes from each other. This is particularly useful for creating complex shapes that would be difficult to model manually. It works by using operations like union, difference, and intersection.

The Mirror Modifier mirrors a mesh along a chosen axis. This is especially useful for symmetric models like characters or vehicles, where you only need to model one half, and the modifier creates the other.

The Bevel Modifier adds beveled edges to a model. This is useful for adding realism, as most real-world objects do not have perfectly sharp edges. The modifier allows for control over the bevel size and shape.

The Solidify Modifier adds thickness to a mesh. This is useful for creating hollow objects or giving depth to otherwise flat surfaces, like cloth or paper.

The Cloth Modifier simulates cloth-like behavior on a mesh. It can be used to create realistic clothing, flags, or any other fabric dynamics in a scene.

The Particle System Modifier allows objects to emit particles. These can be used for creating effects like rain, smoke, fire, or even crowds.

The Displace Modifier displaces a mesh based on a texture. This can be used to create terrain, wrinkles, or other detailed surface effects.

The Lattice Modifier deforms the entire mesh using a simple lattice structure. This is a very powerful tool for making broad, smooth deformations that would be difficult to achieve with normal modeling techniques.

The Decimate Modifier reduces the number of polygons in a mesh. This is useful for creating low-poly models or optimizing models for performance in games or simulations.

Modifiers can be stacked, meaning you can apply multiple modifiers to a single object to achieve complex effects. The order of the modifiers in the stack can affect the final result.

The Armature Modifier is used to deform a mesh based on a skeleton (armature). This is essential for character rigging and animation.

Modifiers can be applied permanently to the mesh, or they can be left active for non-destructive editing. This flexibility allows for continuous adjustments without permanently altering the base geometry.

The Curve Modifier deforms a mesh along a curve. This is useful for creating objects like roads, pipes, or anything that needs to conform to a curved shape.

The Build Modifier creates the effect of building or dismantling an object over time. This can be used for animations where objects appear or disappear.

Modifiers also have settings that can be animated, allowing for dynamic effects in animations.

Blender's Modifier Library is constantly growing, with each new version of Blender often introducing new modifiers, providing even more tools for efficient and creative modeling.

```
# Example Python script to add a modifier to an object in Blender

import bpy

# Select the first object in the scene

obj = bpy.context.scene.objects[0]

# Add a Subdivision Surface modifier

modifier = obj.modifiers.new(name="Subsurf", type='SUBSURF')

modifier.levels = 2
```

```
modifier.render_levels = 3
```

In conclusion, modifiers are an essential part of the Blender modeling toolkit. They provide a way to add complexity and detail to a model, automate repetitive tasks, and allow for flexible, non-destructive editing. Understanding and utilizing modifiers can greatly enhance the efficiency and creativity of your 3D modeling workflow.

2.4 Tips for Creating Realistic Models

Creating realistic models in Blender is a skill that combines technical proficiency with an eye for detail. Here are some tips to enhance the realism of your 3D models.

1. **Reference Images**: Always start with reference images. Whether you're modeling a creature, a car, or a piece of furniture, having real-world references is crucial for accuracy and realism.
2. **Proportions and Scale**: Pay close attention to the proportions and scale of your model. Even slight deviations can make a model look unrealistic. Use Blender's measurement tools to check dimensions and proportions.
3. **Attention to Detail**: Small details can make a big difference. Adding elements like screws, seams, wear and tear, and other small imperfections can greatly enhance realism.
4. **Topology Matters**: For models that need to be animated, topology is key. Ensure that edge loops follow the natural lines of movement, and keep the topology as clean as possible to avoid issues with deformation.
5. **Use High-Resolution Textures**: Textures can make or break the realism of a model. Use high-resolution textures

where possible, and consider using PBR (Physically Based Rendering) materials for more realistic results.

6. **UV Unwrapping**: Properly unwrap your model to ensure textures sit correctly on the surface. Overlapping or stretched UVs can ruin the effect of even the best textures.
7. **Subsurface Scattering**: For organic models like skin, subsurface scattering (SSS) is crucial. It simulates the light passing through translucent materials, like skin, wax, or leaves.
8. **Realistic Lighting**: Lighting has a massive impact on the final look of your model. Use HDRI images for realistic environmental lighting and add key, fill, and backlights where necessary.
9. **Depth of Field**: Using depth of field in your camera settings can add realism, especially for close-up shots. It simulates the natural blurring of objects that are out of the camera's focal range.
10. **Normal and Bump Mapping**: Use normal and bump maps to add surface details without increasing the polygon count of your model. This is especially useful for adding textures like wrinkles, grunge, or wood grain.
11. **Variation in Color and Texture**: In the real world, surfaces are rarely uniform. Add variation to your textures and colors to avoid the 'CGI look'. This can be done through texture painting or procedural textures.
12. **Displacement Maps**: For high-detail models, use displacement maps. These actually alter the geometry of the model based on a texture, allowing for highly detailed surfaces.
13. **Edge Wear and Imperfections**: Adding wear to edges and imperfections can significantly boost realism. This can be done through textures or sculpting.

14. **Reflections and Refractions**: For materials like glass, water, or metal, accurate reflections and refractions are key. Use the correct IOR (Index of Refraction) values and ensure your environment is set up to reflect realistically.
15. **Use Hair and Particle Systems**: For models requiring fur, grass, or other fibrous elements, Blender's particle system can create highly realistic hair and fur.
16. **Rendering Techniques**: Experiment with different rendering techniques like ambient occlusion, bloom, and volumetrics to add depth and realism to your renders.
17. **Post-Processing**: Sometimes, realism is enhanced in post-processing. Use Blender's compositor or external image editing software to adjust color balance, contrast, and add effects like lens flares or vignettes.
18. **Review and Iterate**: Finally, review your model and make iterations. Getting feedback from other artists or comparing your model to the reference images can provide new insights for improvement.

Creating realistic models in Blender is a balance of art and technique. By applying these tips and continually practicing, your ability to create lifelike, detailed models will significantly improve.

2.5 Common Modeling Challenges and Solutions

Modeling in Blender, like any creative process, comes with its set of challenges. Here are some common issues faced by 3D artists and ways to overcome them.

1. **Complex Topology**: Managing complex topology, especially for organic models, can be challenging. To overcome this, use techniques like retopology, where you

create a new, simpler mesh over your detailed sculpt. This simplifies the mesh while retaining the details.

2. **Texture Stretching**: Texture stretching occurs when UV maps are not properly unwrapped. To fix this, spend time correctly unwrapping your UVs, and use Blender's tools like 'Live Unwrap' and 'Minimize Stretch' to optimize the UV layout.
3. **Realistic Texturing**: Achieving realistic textures can be difficult. Utilize high-quality image textures, and combine them with procedural textures in Blender's node editor for more control and detail. Also, consider using PBR materials for more realistic results.
4. **Lighting Challenges**: Proper lighting is crucial for showcasing your models. If you struggle with lighting, start with three-point lighting setups and experiment with HDRIs for environmental lighting. Always consider the interaction of light with your materials.
5. **Proportional Editing Problems**: Sometimes, proportional editing can affect more of the mesh than intended. Use the scroll wheel to adjust the influence radius, and switch between different falloff types to control the effect.
6. **Booleans Creating Messy Topology**: Booleans are great but can create messy topology. To address this, clean up the mesh after using booleans, merging vertices, and correcting edge flow. Consider using the Remesh modifier for a more uniform topology.
7. **Rigging and Deformation Issues**: For models that need to be rigged, incorrect weight painting can lead to bad deformations. Spend time carefully weight painting your model, and use corrective shape keys if necessary.
8. **Slow Performance with High-Poly Models**: High-poly

models can slow down Blender. Use modifiers like Decimate to reduce polygon count or work with a lower-resolution version for the bulk of the modeling, only adding details towards the end.

9. **Modeling Symmetrical Objects**: For symmetrical objects, use the Mirror Modifier to ensure perfect symmetry. Remember to apply the modifier before making asymmetrical changes.
10. **Sharp Edges on Subdivided Models**: Subdivision surfaces can make edges too soft. To maintain sharp edges, use edge creases or add supporting edge loops close to the edges you want to keep sharp.
11. **Difficulties with Organic Shapes**: Organic shapes can be challenging to model. Use sculpting tools for a more intuitive approach, and consider starting with a base mesh to ensure good topology.
12. **Seamless Tiling Textures**: Creating seamless textures can be tricky. Use Blender's texture painting tools to paint over seams or employ external tools designed for texture creation.
13. **Scale and Measurement Issues**: Maintaining correct scale is essential, especially for architectural models. Use Blender's measurement tools and set your scene's units correctly to ensure accurate dimensions.
14. **Particle System Complexity**: Particle systems can be overwhelming. Start with Blender's presets and then tweak the settings. Use weight painting to control the distribution of particles.
15. **Glass and Transparency Rendering**: Rendering realistic glass and transparent materials can be challenging. Ensure you have the correct IOR values, and consider using caustics for more realistic lighting effects.

16. **Animation-Ready Models**: Preparing models for animation requires foresight. Ensure your topology is suitable for deformation, and consider using the Rigify add-on to simplify the rigging process.
17. **Environmental Integration**: Integrating models into environments or photographs requires attention to scale, perspective, and lighting. Use Blender's camera matching tools to align your 3D camera with a background image or photo.
18. **Workflow Efficiency**: Developing an efficient workflow is key. Use custom hotkeys, pie menus, and screen layouts to speed up your process. Blender's ability to customize the interface can be a huge time-saver.
19. **Learning Curve**: Blender has a steep learning curve. Overcome this by breaking down the learning process into manageable chunks, focusing on one aspect of modeling at a time, and using online resources and tutorials.

In 3D modeling, challenges are opportunities for growth and learning. By facing and overcoming these common issues, you can improve your skills and become a more proficient Blender user.

Chapter 3: The Art of Texturing and Materials

3.1 Understanding Textures and Materials in Blender

Texturing and material creation in Blender is a critical process in bringing your 3D models to life. It involves applying colors, patterns, and surface properties to 3D objects to make them look realistic or stylized, depending on the artist's intent.

Materials in Blender are what define the appearance of your objects. They can include colors, textures, and reflectivity, among other properties. Blender's material system is highly flexible and allows for the creation of a wide range of materials.

Textures are images or procedural patterns that are used to add detail to materials. They can be used for color (diffuse), bumpiness (normal), reflectivity (specular), and many other aspects of a material.

The Node Editor in Blender is a powerful tool for creating and editing materials. It provides a visual interface where you can connect different nodes to create complex materials.

Diffuse textures are the most basic type of texture, used to define the color of an object. These can be either image textures (like photographs) or procedural textures generated within Blender.

Specular and Glossiness maps control the reflective properties of a material. They define which parts of the object are shiny and how shiny they are. These are important for creating materials like metals and plastics.

Normal maps are used to simulate high levels of detail without increasing the model's polygon count. They give the illusion of depth on a flat surface by altering the way light interacts with it.

Bump maps are similar to normal maps but are simpler and affect the surface shading rather than the light reflection. They are useful for adding surface details like scratches, dents, or grooves.

Displacement maps physically displace the mesh to which they're applied, based on the texture. They are used for adding high levels of detail to a surface.

Transparency and Opacity maps are used to create materials like glass or water. They define which parts of an object are transparent and how transparent they are.

Emission maps make parts of your object emit light. This is useful for creating things like screens, lightbulbs, or glowing elements in a scene.

UV mapping is the process of projecting your 3D model onto a 2D plane for texturing. Proper UV mapping is essential for accurately applying image textures to your model.

Procedural textures are generated mathematically within Blender and provide a high level of control and flexibility. They can be used to create organic patterns like wood grain, marble, or clouds.

Texture painting allows you to paint textures directly onto your 3D model. This gives you artistic freedom to create detailed and unique textures.

The Principled BSDF shader in Blender is a versatile shader node used for creating a wide variety of materials. It simplifies the process of shader creation by combining multiple aspects into a single node.

For realism, understanding how light interacts with different materials is key. Study real-world materials and how they look under different lighting conditions.

Environment textures can add realism to your scenes by providing realistic lighting and reflections. These are typically high-dynamic-range images (HDRIs) that encapsulate a 360-degree view of a scene.

Blender also offers options for fine-tuning materials with settings for anisotropy, sheen, clearcoat, and subsurface scattering, each adding another level of realism to materials.

```
# Example Python script to create a simple material in Blender

import bpy

# Create a new material

material = bpy.data.materials.new(name="SimpleMaterial")

material.use_nodes = True

# Get the material's node tree

nodes = material.node_tree.nodes

# Clear existing nodes

for node in nodes:

nodes.remove(node)

# Create a Principled BSDF shader node

principled_node = nodes.new(type='ShaderNodeBsdfPrincipled')

principled_node.location = (0, 0)
```

```
# Create an Output node

output_node = nodes.new('ShaderNodeOutputMaterial')

output_node.location = (200, 0)

# Link Principled BSDF to Output

material.node_tree.links.new(principled_node.outputs['BSDF'], output_node.inputs['Surface'])

# Set some properties of the Principled BSDF

principled_node.inputs['Base Color'].default_value = (0.8, 0.3, 0.3, 1) # RGB and Alpha

principled_node.inputs['Roughness'].default_value = 0.5
```

Understanding and effectively using textures and materials is crucial in the creation of visually appealing 3D art. The right combination of textures and materials can bring a model to life, adding depth, realism, or artistic flair to your projects.

3.2 Creating Your Own Textures: A Step-by-Step Guide

Creating your own textures in Blender is a rewarding process that allows for a high degree of customization and creativity. Here's a step-by-step guide to creating textures in Blender.

1. **Start with a Plan**: Before you begin, have a clear idea of what texture you want to create. Gather reference images if you're aiming for realism, or sketch out ideas if you're creating something from your imagination.
2. **Setting Up Your Workspace**: Open Blender and set up

your workspace for texture creation. This typically involves opening the UV/Image Editor and the 3D Viewport side by side.

3. **Preparing Your Model for Texturing**: If you're applying the texture to a model, ensure it's UV unwrapped. UV unwrapping is the process of laying out the 3D model in a 2D space to apply the texture accurately.
4. **Creating a New Texture**: In the UV/Image Editor, create a new image to be used as the texture. Set the resolution high to ensure good quality, but be mindful of your system's limitations.
5. **Texture Painting**: Switch to Texture Paint mode in the 3D Viewport. Here, you can paint directly onto your 3D model. Blender offers various brushes and settings to simulate different texture effects.
6. **Using Layers**: Just like in image editing software, you can use layers in your texture painting process. This allows for non-destructive editing and more control over the final look.
7. **Incorporating Images**: You can also use existing images as part of your texture. These can be photographs, graphics, or any image. Import them into Blender and use them as stencils or directly map them onto the model.
8. **Procedural Texturing**: Blender's procedural texturing capabilities are vast. You can use nodes to create textures from scratch, offering endless possibilities. Experiment with different nodes to create unique textures.
9. **Fine-Tuning in the Shader Editor**: For further refinement of your texture, switch to the Shader Editor. Here you can adjust how the texture interacts with light and the material properties of your model.
10. **Baking Textures**: Once your texture is ready, you can bake

it onto your model. This process converts all the texture information into image files that can be used in other software or game engines.

11. **Exporting Textures**: If you need to use the texture outside Blender, you can export it. Go to the UV/Image Editor, select your texture, and save it in your desired format.
12. **Testing Your Texture**: Apply your texture to your model and render it to see how it looks. Check it under different lighting conditions and from various angles.
13. **Adjustments and Iterations**: Often, your first attempt may not be perfect. Don't hesitate to go back and make adjustments to your texture as needed.
14. **Adding Multiple Textures**: For more complex materials, you might need multiple textures like diffuse, specular, normal, or bump maps. Create these using the same process and combine them using Blender's material nodes.
15. **Consider Physical Properties**: When creating textures, consider the physical properties of the material you're emulating. How does it react to light? Does it have a rough or smooth surface? These considerations will guide your texturing process.
16. **Using Texture Masks**: Masks can be used to control where certain textures or colors appear on your model. This can be especially useful for adding wear and tear or dirt to specific areas.
17. **Layering Effects**: For added complexity, layer different effects on top of each other. For instance, a rust texture can be layered over a metal texture to create an aged metal effect.
18. **Real-World Testing**: If possible, test how your texture looks in a real-world setting or game engine. This can provide insights into how it performs under different

conditions.

19. **Organizing Your Textures**: Keep your textures organized, especially if you're working on a large project. Proper naming and storage will save you time in the long run.
20. **Continuous Learning**: Texture creation is a vast field, and there's always something new to learn. Keep experimenting and learning new techniques to improve your skills.

Creating textures in Blender is a mix of art and technique. With practice, you can create textures that add realism and depth to your models, making them stand out.

3.3 Using UV Mapping for Accurate Texture Placement

UV mapping is a crucial step in the texturing process, ensuring that your textures align correctly with your 3D models. Here's a comprehensive guide on how to effectively use UV mapping in Blender.

1. **Understanding UV Mapping**: UV mapping involves unwrapping a 3D model onto a 2D surface to allow for accurate texture placement. The 'U' and 'V' refer to the axis of the 2D texture plane, analogous to the X and Y axis in 3D space.
2. **Marking Seams**: Before unwrapping, you need to mark seams on your model. Seams are like cuts that determine how the model unfolds onto the 2D plane. Choose seams in areas that are less noticeable or where natural seams would occur in real life.
3. **Unwrapping Your Model**: After marking seams, select your model and unwrap it by pressing U and choosing an unwrap method. Blender offers several unwrapping

methods, including Smart UV Project, which can be useful for objects with less organic shapes.

4. **Inspecting the UV Layout**: Once unwrapped, the UV layout is displayed in the UV/Image Editor. Ensure that the layout makes efficient use of the space and that there's minimal stretching.
5. **Adjusting the UVs**: If there are issues with the UV layout, you can manually adjust it in the UV/Image Editor. You can move, scale, and rotate the UVs to better fit the texture space.
6. **Using UV Squares for Alignment**: For objects with straight edges or geometric patterns, use the UV Squares addon to align your UVs in straight lines. This ensures that textures like bricks or tiles align correctly.
7. **Dealing with Overlapping UVs**: Overlapping UVs can be useful for mirrored textures but can cause problems in other cases. Ensure that your UVs are not overlapping unintentionally, as this will cause the texture to repeat in those areas.
8. **Texture Painting with UVs**: UV maps can also be used as a guide for texture painting. You can export the UV layout and use it in an image editing software to create textures that align perfectly with your model.
9. **Minimizing Stretching**: To minimize stretching, use the 'Minimize Stretch' tool in the UV/Image Editor. This tool adjusts the UVs to reduce distortion in the texture.
10. **Pinning UVs for Complex Models**: For more complex models, you can pin certain UVs in place. This is useful when making adjustments to the rest of the UV map, as the pinned UVs will remain stationary.
11. **Live Unwrap for Interactive Adjustments**: Blender's Live Unwrap feature allows you to see changes in the UV layout

in real-time as you adjust seams on your model. This can speed up the process of finding the optimal unwrap.

12. **Using Proportional Editing in UV Space**: Proportional editing can also be used in the UV/Image Editor. This is useful for making broad adjustments to the UVs while maintaining a level of uniformity.
13. **UV Mapping for Games**: When UV mapping for game assets, be mindful of texture size and texel density. Consistent texel density ensures that textures appear uniform across different objects.
14. **UV Mapping Non-Standard Objects**: For objects that don't unwrap well with standard methods, consider using projective unwrapping methods like Project From View or Cube Projection.
15. **Exporting UV Layouts**: You can export your UV layout from Blender to use as a template in texture creation software. This helps in creating textures that fit perfectly with your model.
16. **Organizing UV Maps for Multiple Textures**: If your model uses multiple textures, organize your UV maps accordingly. Blender allows for multiple UV maps on a single model, which can be assigned to different textures.
17. **Testing Textures with UV Maps**: Always test your textures with the UV map applied to ensure they align correctly on the model. Adjust the UV map as necessary to achieve the best result.
18. **Learning from Real-World Examples**: Look at how fabrics, labels, and other materials are applied in the real world for inspiration on how to effectively UV map your models.
19. **Continuous Practice**: Mastering UV mapping takes practice. Experiment with different models and unwrap

methods to improve your skills.

UV mapping is a critical skill in 3D modeling and texturing, allowing for precise control over how textures are applied to models. With practice, it becomes an invaluable tool in creating professional and realistic 3D art.

3.4 Exploring Shaders and Material Nodes

Shaders and material nodes in Blender are essential tools for creating detailed and realistic materials. They provide a way to define how surfaces interact with light and shadow, giving life to 3D models.

1. **Understanding Shaders**: Shaders in Blender are used to determine how materials look under different lighting conditions. The most commonly used shader in Blender is the Principled BSDF, which simulates a wide range of materials.
2. **Node-Based Material System**: Blender uses a node-based system for materials. This means you can create materials by connecting different types of nodes in a network, providing enormous flexibility and control.
3. **Principled BSDF Shader**: The Principled BSDF is a versatile shader designed to simulate a variety of materials like plastics, metals, glass, and fabrics. It includes parameters like roughness, metallic, transmission, and subsurface scattering.
4. **Using Textures with Shaders**: Textures can be connected to shaders to add details like color variation, bumpiness, and reflectivity. Image textures can be used, or procedural textures can be generated within Blender.
5. **Layering Materials with Mix Shader**: The Mix Shader node allows you to blend two different shaders together.

This can be used to create complex materials with layered properties.

6. **Creating Transparent Materials**: The Transparency Shader is used to create transparent materials like glass or water. It can be mixed with other shaders for more complex effects like frosted glass.
7. **Emission for Light-Emitting Materials**: The Emission Shader makes materials emit light. This is useful for creating objects like light bulbs, screens, or glowing elements.
8. **Bump and Normal Maps for Surface Details**: Bump and Normal Maps can be used with shaders to simulate detailed surface textures without adding extra geometry to the model.
9. **Subsurface Scattering for Organic Materials**: Subsurface Scattering (SSS) simulates light penetrating semi-transparent materials. This is crucial for realistic skin, wax, and other organic materials.
10. **Utilizing Ambient Occlusion**: Ambient Occlusion nodes can add depth to crevices and corners, enhancing the realism of textures and materials.
11. **Displacement for Realistic Textures**: The Displacement node alters the geometry of the surface based on a texture, adding realistic depth to materials like stone or wood.
12. **Non-Photorealistic Rendering with Toon Shader**: The Toon Shader provides a way to create stylized, non-photorealistic materials suitable for cartoons or anime.
13. **Working with Fresnel and Layer Weight**: These nodes control how light reflects at different angles, essential for creating materials like car paint or certain types of plastics.
14. **Color Ramp for Gradients and Transitions**: The Color Ramp node is used to create gradients and control

transitions between different colors in a material.

15. **Using Math Nodes for Advanced Control**: Math nodes can be used to manipulate values within a material, giving you precise control over various aspects of how it appears.
16. **Animating Material Properties**: Almost every aspect of a shader can be animated in Blender, allowing for dynamic changes in materials over time.
17. **Custom Shader Creation with OSL**: For advanced users, Blender offers support for Open Shading Language (OSL), which lets you write your custom shaders.
18. **Optimizing Materials for Rendering**: While creating complex materials, it's important to consider render times. Optimizing node setups can help reduce rendering times without compromising quality.
19. **Testing and Iteration**: Creating materials often requires trial and error. Experiment with different node setups and test renders to achieve the desired result.
20. **Learning from Presets and Examples**: Blender comes with a variety of material presets. Studying these can provide insights into how different node setups work.

By mastering shaders and material nodes, you can create a wide range of realistic and stylized materials, greatly enhancing the visual appeal of your 3D projects.

3.5 Realistic Texturing: From Theory to Practice

Realistic texturing is a critical skill in 3D modeling, as it brings a level of authenticity and life to your creations. This section explores the transition from understanding texturing theory to practical application in Blender.

1. **Analyzing Real-World Materials**: Start by closely observing real-world materials. Note their color variations, surface imperfections, and how they react to light. These observations are crucial for creating realistic textures.
2. **Gathering Reference Images**: Collect high-quality images of the material you aim to recreate. These will serve as a guide for color, pattern, and detail in your textures.
3. **Understanding PBR Workflow**: Physically Based Rendering (PBR) is a methodology in texturing that aims to create materials that accurately react to light. It involves using specific maps like albedo, roughness, metallic, and normal maps.
4. **Creating Base Textures**: Start by creating the base color (albedo) texture. This texture should represent the color of the material without any lighting or shadow effects.
5. **Adding Detail with Bump and Normal Maps**: Use bump and normal maps to add surface details. These maps simulate the small surface irregularities that are essential for realism.
6. **Using Roughness and Specular Maps**: Roughness and specular maps define how shiny or matte a surface is and how it reflects light. These are key to creating materials like metals, plastics, or glass.
7. **Incorporating Ambient Occlusion**: Ambient occlusion adds depth and realism by simulating the way light behaves in crevices and corners. It can be baked from a high-poly model or painted manually.
8. **Implementing Displacement Maps for Depth**: For textures requiring significant depth, like rocky surfaces or engraved details, use displacement maps. These maps alter the geometry based on the texture.
9. **Balancing Detail and Performance**: Higher detail often

means more complex textures and longer render times. Find a balance by focusing detail where it's most visible and optimizing textures for performance.

10. **Utilizing Procedural Textures**: Blender's procedural textures can be used to create patterns and details without image textures. These can be combined with image-based textures for more complex materials.
11. **Layering Textures for Complexity**: Real-world materials often have layers of different textures. Use Blender's material nodes to layer different textures and create complex materials.
12. **Texture Painting for Custom Details**: For unique or specific details, texture painting allows you to paint directly onto the model. This is useful for adding wear, tear, dirt, or specific patterns.
13. **Testing in Different Lighting Conditions**: Materials can look vastly different under various lighting. Test your textures under multiple lighting setups to ensure they maintain realism.
14. **Using HDRI for Environment Reflections**: HDRI images provide realistic environmental reflections and lighting. They are particularly useful for reflective materials like metals or glass.
15. **Fine-Tuning in the Shader Editor**: Use the Shader Editor to fine-tune your materials. Adjust node settings and combine different shaders to achieve the desired result.
16. **Learning from Real-life Examples**: Apply what you learn by attempting to recreate materials from objects around you. This practical application solidifies your understanding and skills.
17. **Staying Organized with Node Groups**: Complex materials can lead to cluttered node setups. Use node

groups to keep your Shader Editor organized.

18. **Experimentation and Iteration**: Experiment with different settings and techniques. Texturing is often a process of trial and error, and frequent iteration can lead to better results.
19. **Seeking Feedback and Critique**: Share your work with others and seek feedback. Constructive critique is invaluable for learning and improvement.
20. **Continuous Learning and Adaptation**: Stay updated with new techniques and tools in texturing. The field is always evolving, and continuous learning is key to staying proficient.

By applying these practices, you can bridge the gap between theoretical knowledge and practical application, leading to the creation of highly realistic textures in your 3D projects.

Chapter 4: Lighting and Rendering

4.1 Basics of Lighting in 3D Environments

Lighting is a fundamental aspect of 3D rendering, playing a crucial role in defining the mood, atmosphere, and realism of a scene. Understanding the basics of lighting in Blender is essential for any 3D artist.

1. **Types of Lights**: Blender offers several types of lights - Point, Sun, Spot, and Area. Each has its unique characteristics and uses. Point lights emit light in all directions, Sun lights simulate sunlight with parallel rays, Spotlights emit light in a cone shape, and Area lights are great for soft, diffused lighting.
2. **Understanding Light Properties**: Each light type in Blender has different properties like color, intensity, and size. Tweaking these properties helps in achieving the desired effect in your scene.
3. **The Role of Color in Lighting**: Light color significantly affects the mood of a scene. Warmer tones generally convey comfort and intimacy, while cooler tones can create a more distant or eerie atmosphere.
4. **Three-Point Lighting**: A fundamental lighting setup is the three-point lighting system, which includes a key light, fill light, and back light. This setup is versatile and can be used for a variety of scenes to provide depth and dimension.
5. **Key Light**: The key light is the main light source and is typically the strongest. It defines the most visible lighting and shadow patterns on the subject.
6. **Fill Light**: The fill light is used to lighten the shadows created by the key light. It is usually less intense and placed

on the opposite side of the key light.

7. **Back Light**: The back light, or rim light, is placed behind the subject. It helps in separating the subject from the background and adds a sense of depth.
8. **Ambient Lighting**: Ambient lighting provides general illumination to a scene. It's non-directional and helps in softening shadows and revealing details.
9. **Using HDRI for Environmental Lighting**: HDRIs (High Dynamic Range Images) are used to create realistic environmental lighting. They can provide a natural and complex light setup with minimal effort.
10. **Shadows and Their Importance**: Shadows are crucial for adding realism and depth. Blender allows control over shadow softness, color, and strength, which can greatly affect the mood and realism of the scene.
11. **Lighting for Different Times of Day**: The color and direction of light change throughout the day. Mimic these changes in your scene to depict different times of day accurately.
12. **Effect of Light Size**: The size of the light source affects the softness of the shadows. Larger light sources produce softer shadows, while smaller sources create sharper shadows.
13. **Utilizing Spotlights for Focus**: Spotlights are excellent for drawing attention to specific areas or objects in your scene, creating a focal point.
14. **Light Falloff and Distance**: Understanding how light intensity decreases with distance (falloff) is key for setting up realistic lighting.
15. **Rendering Preview and Adjustments**: Use Blender's real-time rendering viewport to preview lighting changes and make adjustments on the fly.
16. **Layering Lights for Complexity**: Layering multiple lights

can add complexity and richness to your scene. Experiment with different colors and intensities for a dynamic look.

17. **Balancing Realism and Artistic Intent**: Sometimes, you may need to deviate from realistic lighting to achieve a specific artistic effect. Understanding the basics allows you to bend the rules effectively.
18. **Learning from Real-life Examples**: Study how light behaves in real life and try to replicate similar conditions in your 3D scenes. This practice can significantly improve your lighting skills.
19. **Continuous Experimentation**: Experiment with different lighting setups and observe how they affect your scene. Each project can be an opportunity to try something new.
20. **Keeping Performance in Mind**: High-quality lighting can be render-intensive. Balance the quality with render times, especially for animations or complex scenes.

Mastering the basics of lighting in 3D environments is a continuous learning process, requiring practice and experimentation. Effective lighting can elevate the visual appeal of your scenes, making them more dynamic and engaging.

4.2 Mastering Blender's Rendering Engines: Cycles and Eevee

Blender offers two primary rendering engines, Cycles and Eevee, each with its unique strengths and applications. Understanding how to utilize these engines effectively is crucial for any 3D artist.

1. **Cycles Overview**: Cycles is Blender's ray-trace based rendering engine. It calculates the way light interacts with objects in a physically accurate way, producing highly realistic images. It's ideal for projects where photorealism is

the goal.

2. **Eevee Overview**: Eevee is Blender's real-time render engine. It uses rasterization instead of ray tracing, which allows for much faster rendering times. While it may not achieve the same level of realism as Cycles, Eevee is excellent for quick previews and animations.
3. **Choosing Between Cycles and Eevee**: The choice between Cycles and Eevee depends on your project's needs. If time is not a constraint and you need photorealistic renders, Cycles is the way to go. For faster renders and a more interactive experience, Eevee is preferable.
4. **Lighting in Cycles vs. Eevee**: Lighting behaves differently in each engine. Cycles provides more realistic lighting and shadows, but at the cost of longer render times. Eevee, being faster, may require additional setup for similar results.
5. **Materials and Textures**: Both engines use the same material and texture setup, but they can render differently. Some advanced Cycles features like subsurface scattering or volumetrics might have limitations or different appearances in Eevee.
6. **Render Settings in Cycles**: In Cycles, settings like sample count, light paths, and bounces significantly affect render quality and time. Higher samples and more light bounces result in better quality but longer render times.
7. **Render Settings in Eevee**: In Eevee, settings like screen space reflections, shadows, and indirect light play a crucial role. Eevee also supports features like bloom, ambient occlusion, and depth of field directly in the render engine.
8. **Using HDRI in Both Engines**: HDRI lighting works well with both Cycles and Eevee. However, Eevee might require additional light probes to accurately capture environmental

lighting.

9. **Optimizing Renders in Cycles**: For faster renders in Cycles, reduce the number of light bounces, lower the sample count, and use denoising features to clean up the noise.
10. **Optimizing Renders in Eevee**: In Eevee, optimizing render times can involve reducing the resolution of shadows, turning off screen space reflections, or lowering the subdivision level of objects.
11. **Camera Settings**: Camera settings like depth of field and motion blur are handled differently in each engine. Cycles calculates these effects physically, while Eevee provides more performance-friendly solutions.
12. **Using Bake Features**: For static scenes, you can bake lighting and shadows in Cycles to textures, which can then be used in Eevee for faster renders.
13. **Animation Considerations**: For animations, Eevee is often preferred due to its faster render times. However, Cycles can provide a higher quality result for final renders.
14. **Testing and Previewing**: Regular testing and previewing in both engines is essential to understand how your scene will render. This can help in making adjustments specific to each engine.
15. **Utilizing GPU and CPU Rendering**: Cycles supports both GPU and CPU rendering. GPU rendering is generally faster, but CPU can be more effective for scenes with high memory requirements.
16. **Noise Reduction in Cycles**: Noise can be a challenge in Cycles, especially in low-light conditions. Use denoising tools in Blender to mitigate this issue.
17. **Balancing Quality and Speed**: Finding the right balance between render quality and speed is key. Experiment with

different settings to find what works best for your project and hardware.

18. **Learning from Tutorials and Community**: Engaging with the Blender community and learning from tutorials can provide valuable insights into effectively using both rendering engines.
19. **Continuous Experimentation**: Experimentation is vital. Try different settings, lighting setups, and materials in both engines to understand their capabilities and limitations.
20. **Staying Updated**: Both Cycles and Eevee are continuously being developed. Stay updated with the latest features and improvements to make the most out of these powerful rendering engines.

Mastering Cycles and Eevee in Blender opens up a world of possibilities for rendering high-quality 3D images and animations. By understanding the strengths and limitations of each engine, you can choose the right tool for your specific needs and achieve the best possible results.

4.3 Photorealistic Rendering: Techniques and Tips

Achieving photorealistic rendering in Blender requires a combination of technical skills, artistic vision, and attention to detail. Here are some techniques and tips to help you create renders that closely mimic real life.

1. **Understanding Real-World Physics**: The key to photorealism is understanding how light and materials interact in the real world. Study the principles of light, reflection, refraction, and shadow in different environments.

2. **High-Quality Textures**: Use high-resolution textures for more detail. Textures not only add color but also contribute to the materiality of objects, like roughness, glossiness, and bump.
3. **Accurate Material Properties**: Use physically accurate materials. This involves setting up shaders that mimic real-world properties, using nodes like the Principled BSDF in Blender for realistic materials.
4. **Subsurface Scattering for Organic Materials**: For materials like skin, wax, and leaves, subsurface scattering (SSS) is crucial to achieve a realistic look, as it simulates light passing through translucent materials.
5. **Realistic Lighting Setup**: Mimic real-world lighting conditions. Use HDRIs for natural environmental lighting and set up artificial lights like in real-life scenarios.
6. **Depth of Field**: Use depth of field to mimic the way cameras focus on an object, creating a blurred background or foreground that adds to the realism.
7. **Camera Settings and Composition**: Just like in photography, the composition and camera settings play a crucial role. Adjust the focal length, aperture, and shutter speed to mimic real camera effects.
8. **Attention to Detail**: Pay attention to small details in your scene. Adding imperfections like scratches, dents, and dust can make your render more realistic.
9. **Post-Processing**: Use post-processing techniques to adjust the final image. This can include color correction, adjusting contrast, adding vignettes, or even adding lens flares.
10. **Rendering Settings**: In Cycles, use a higher number of samples for less noise. Consider using denoising algorithms to clean up the image while keeping render times reasonable.

11. **Use of Global Illumination**: Global Illumination (GI) simulates the way light bounces off surfaces and affects the overall illumination. Ensure GI is enabled for a more realistic light setup.
12. **Realistic Environment Setup**: Create an environment that complements your model. This includes setting up realistic backgrounds, floors, and surrounding objects.
13. **Reflective and Transparent Surfaces**: Pay special attention to reflective and transparent surfaces as they can significantly add to the realism through reflections and light transmission.
14. **Balancing Performance and Quality**: Photorealistic rendering can be resource-intensive. Balance the render quality with the capabilities of your hardware, optimizing where necessary.
15. **Use of Ambient Occlusion**: Ambient occlusion can add depth to crevices and corners, enhancing the realism of the textures and overall scene.
16. **Regular Testing and Previewing**: Constantly test and preview your renders. This helps in making incremental adjustments and catching any issues early in the process.
17. **Studying Real-Life Examples**: Continuously observe and study real-life examples and try to replicate them in Blender. This practice improves your understanding of how to achieve photorealism.
18. **Experimentation and Patience**: Achieving photorealism is often a trial-and-error process. Be patient and willing to experiment with different settings and techniques.
19. **Learning from the Community**: Engage with the Blender community, follow tutorials, and learn from the work of others. Often, insights from other artists can provide new perspectives and techniques.

20. **Staying Updated with Technology**: Keep up-to-date with the latest advancements in rendering technology. New updates in Blender often come with improved features that can enhance photorealism.

By applying these techniques and continually refining your skills, you can create stunning, photorealistic renders in Blender that are indistinguishable from real-life photographs.

4.4 Optimizing Render Settings for Quality and Speed

Optimizing render settings in Blender is crucial for achieving a balance between image quality and rendering speed. Here are some key strategies and tips for optimizing your rendering workflow.

1. **Understanding Render Engines**: Choose the right render engine for your project. Cycles is better for photorealistic results, while Eevee is faster and more suitable for real-time rendering.
2. **Sample Rate Adjustment**: In Cycles, adjust the sample rate according to the complexity of your scene. Higher samples increase quality but also render time. Use lower samples for test renders.
3. **Utilizing Denoising**: Use denoising tools to reduce noise in your renders. This allows you to use lower sample rates without significantly compromising the quality.
4. **Light Bounces Optimization**: Reducing the number of light bounces can decrease render times. Adjust the number of bounces in the render settings, keeping them as low as possible without sacrificing too much realism.
5. **Managing Resolution**: Lower the resolution for test renders. Full resolution is only necessary for final renders,

and lower resolutions can significantly speed up testing.

6. **Render Layers and Passes**: Use render layers and passes to split your scene into manageable parts. This not only speeds up rendering but also provides more control in post-processing.
7. **Optimizing Textures and Materials**: Large textures can slow down renders. Use appropriately sized textures and optimize material node setups to improve render efficiency.
8. **Using Simplified Geometry**: Where detail is not critical, use simplified geometry. This is particularly effective for background elements.
9. **Efficient Lighting**: Excessive or inefficient lighting can increase render times. Use the minimum number of lights necessary and optimize their settings for performance.
10. **Viewport Rendering for Previews**: Use viewport rendering for quick previews. This can give you a good idea of how your final render will look without the time investment of a full render.
11. **Optimizing Shadow Settings**: Shadows can be render-intensive. Adjust shadow settings like size and softness, and disable them where they are not needed.
12. **Managing Ray Visibility**: In complex scenes, manage ray visibility settings for objects. Disable ray visibility for reflections, shadows, or transmission where it doesn't affect the scene's visual quality.
13. **Using Baking Techniques**: Bake lighting and textures for static objects. This can drastically reduce rendering times, especially for scenes with complex lighting.
14. **GPU and CPU Rendering**: Choose between GPU and CPU rendering based on your hardware. GPUs generally offer faster rendering for Cycles, but CPU might be more effective for certain scenes.

15. **Compositing for Efficiency**: Use Blender's compositing features to combine passes or add effects. This can be more efficient than trying to achieve everything in a single render pass.
16. **Using Add-ons for Optimization**: Consider using add-ons designed to help optimize rendering, such as those that manage complex node setups or streamline scene settings.
17. **Batch Rendering for Multiple Images**: For multiple images, such as animations or variations of a scene, use batch rendering. This automates the process and can be more efficient than rendering each image individually.
18. **Regular Software Updates**: Keep Blender updated. New versions often include optimizations and new features that can improve rendering performance.
19. **Testing and Experimentation**: Regularly test different settings to find the best balance for your specific project. Each scene is unique and may require different optimizations.
20. **Learning from the Community**: Stay engaged with the Blender community. Tips and tricks shared by other artists can be invaluable in finding new ways to optimize your render settings.

By fine-tuning these aspects of your rendering setup, you can significantly improve rendering times while maintaining high-quality results, allowing for a more efficient and productive 3D workflow.

4.5 Post-Processing and Compositing in Blender

Post-processing and compositing are essential steps in the 3D rendering process, allowing you to enhance and refine your rendered images. Blender offers a range of tools and techniques for effective post-processing.

1. **Understanding the Compositor**: Blender's compositor is a powerful tool for post-processing your renders. It works with nodes, similar to material and texture setups, offering a non-destructive workflow.
2. **Using Render Layers and Passes**: Render your scene in layers and passes for greater control in post-processing. This allows you to adjust, combine, or enhance different elements of your scene independently.
3. **Color Correction**: Adjust the color balance, brightness, contrast, and saturation of your image in the compositor. This can greatly improve the overall look of your render.
4. **Adding Effects with Nodes**: Utilize various nodes in the compositor to add effects like glare, bloom, lens flares, or vignettes. These effects can add a cinematic quality to your renders.
5. **Combining Render Passes**: Blend different render passes like shadows, specular highlights, or ambient occlusion for more nuanced control over lighting and detail.
6. **Using the Glare Node for Realism**: The Glare node can be used to simulate realistic lens effects, such as bloom around bright light sources, enhancing the realism of your scene.
7. **Depth of Field and Bokeh Effects**: If you didn't use depth of field in your camera settings, you could add or enhance it in post-processing for a more dramatic or realistic effect.

8. **Adding Motion Blur**: Add motion blur in post-processing for dynamic scenes. This is particularly useful for animations where motion blur can add a sense of speed and motion.
9. **Chroma Keying for Background Replacement**: Use chroma keying in the compositor to replace backgrounds or combine your 3D renders with real-life footage.
10. **Noise Reduction in Post**: If your render has noise, additional noise reduction can be applied in the compositor, often with more control than during rendering.
11. **Creating Atmosphere with Fog or Mist**: Use the Z-pass to create atmospheric effects like fog or mist, adding depth and ambiance to your scene.
12. **Adjusting Material Properties**: If certain material properties didn't render as expected, you could make adjustments or enhancements to them in post-processing.
13. **Using Alpha Over for Layering**: The Alpha Over node is useful for layering different elements of your scene, such as foreground objects or particle effects.
14. **Masking for Selective Adjustments**: Create masks to make selective adjustments to your render, like brightening a specific part of the image or adding color to a particular object.
15. **Grading for Mood and Style**: Apply color grading to set the mood or style of your render. This can range from subtle adjustments to create a specific time of day to more stylized looks like a vintage or noir effect.
16. **Utilizing MultiLayer OpenEXR for Flexibility**: Render your scene in MultiLayer OpenEXR format to retain the highest quality and flexibility for post-processing.
17. **Sharpening for Final Polish**: Apply sharpening filters to

enhance the clarity and crispness of your render.

18. **Creating Custom Node Setups**: You can create custom node setups for effects that you use frequently, saving them as node groups for reuse in future projects.
19. **Rendering in Layers for Complex Scenes**: For complex scenes, rendering in layers and compositing them together can be more manageable and less memory-intensive than rendering the whole scene at once.
20. **Experimenting and Learning**: Post-processing is an area ripe for experimentation. Try different node combinations and settings to discover new effects and improve your skills.

By mastering post-processing and compositing in Blender, you can significantly enhance the quality of your renders, bringing them closer to your artistic vision.

Chapter 5: Animation and Rigging

5.1 Introduction to Animation in Blender

Animation in Blender is a powerful tool, allowing artists to bring their creations to life. Understanding the basics of animation is essential for anyone looking to explore this dynamic aspect of 3D art.

1. **Keyframe Animation**: The most basic form of animation in Blender involves keyframes. Keyframes are used to define the start and end points of any action in the timeline.
2. **Animating Transform Properties**: You can animate most properties in Blender, but the most common are the transform properties: location, rotation, and scale of an object.
3. **Setting Keyframes**: To set a keyframe, simply position your object at the desired point in time and space, and press 'I' to insert a keyframe. You can choose which property to keyframe, such as location, rotation, or scale.
4. **Timeline and Dope Sheet**: The timeline is where you can scrub through your animation, while the dope sheet provides a more detailed view of your keyframes and allows for more intricate editing.
5. **Interpolation and Easing**: Between keyframes, Blender interpolates the values to create smooth motion. You can adjust this interpolation and apply easing for more dynamic animations.
6. **Graph Editor for Fine-tuning**: The graph editor allows you to adjust the interpolation curves between keyframes. This is useful for refining the timing and flow of your animation.

7. **Animating Materials and Effects**: Besides object properties, you can also animate material properties, like color or opacity, and even particle systems.
8. **Looping Animations**: For actions that need to repeat, like a walk cycle, you can make your animation loopable. This involves careful planning of the start and end keyframes.
9. **Non-Linear Animation (NLA) Editor**: For complex animations, the NLA Editor allows you to layer and blend different actions. This is particularly useful for character animation.
10. **Rigging for Animation**: Before animating characters, you need to rig them. Rigging is the process of creating a skeleton (armature) for your model so it can move in a lifelike way.
11. **Weight Painting for Rigging**: Weight painting is used to define how much influence each bone in the armature has over different parts of the mesh. This is crucial for smooth deformations.
12. **Using Constraints for Controlled Movements**: Constraints can be used to control the behavior of objects during animation. For example, a 'Follow Path' constraint can make an object move along a predefined path.
13. **Principles of Animation**: Understanding the 12 principles of animation, like anticipation, squash and stretch, and timing, is crucial for creating lifelike and appealing animations.
14. **Animation Layers**: Similar to layers in drawing software, animation layers in Blender allow you to work on different aspects of your animation separately, like facial expressions and body movements.
15. **Baking Animations**: Baking animations can be useful for complex simulations like cloth or physics, where you want

to convert the simulation into keyframes.

16. **Motion Paths for Visualization**: Use motion paths to visualize the trajectory of an object or character over time. This helps in planning and refining movements.
17. **Camera Animation for Dynamic Shots**: Animating the camera can add dynamism to your scene. Keyframe the camera's position, rotation, and even focal length for cinematic effects.
18. **Rendering Animations**: When rendering animations, consider factors like frame rate, output format, and render quality. Remember that rendering animations can be time-consuming.
19. **Practice and Experimentation**: Like any art form, animation requires practice. Experiment with different types of animation to find your preferred style and improve your skills.
20. **Learning from Resources and the Community**: Utilize the vast array of online tutorials, courses, and community forums dedicated to Blender animation to enhance your learning experience.

Animation in Blender opens up a world of possibilities for storytelling and creative expression. By understanding and mastering the basics, you can start bringing your 3D models to life with engaging and dynamic animations.

5.2 Rigging 101: Preparing Your Model for Animation

Rigging is a crucial process in animation, involving the creation of a skeleton or structure that controls the movement of a 3D model. This section delves into the fundamentals of rigging in Blender.

1. **Understanding Armatures**: In Blender, the rigging system is based on armatures, which are essentially skeletons made of bones. These bones are used to control the movement of a model.
2. **Creating a Basic Armature**: Start by adding an armature to your scene. This can be done through the Add menu. Position the first bone at the base of your model, typically the hips or pelvis for characters.
3. **Editing Bone Structure**: Enter Edit Mode to edit the structure of your armature. You can extrude bones from existing ones to create a full skeleton that matches the anatomy of your model.
4. **Naming Bones for Clarity**: Properly name your bones for clarity and ease of use, especially in complex rigs. Names like 'LeftArm' or 'RightLeg' are standard practices.
5. **Parenting Mesh to Armature**: Once your armature is complete, parent your mesh to the armature. This can be done with automatic weights, which Blender uses to guess how much each bone should influence different parts of the mesh.
6. **Weight Painting for Accuracy**: After automatic weights are applied, you'll likely need to fine-tune the influence of each bone on the mesh. This is done through weight painting, where red indicates high influence and blue indicates low influence.
7. **Adding Inverse Kinematics (IK) for Realistic Movement**: IK is a technique used in rigging to allow for more natural movement, particularly in limbs. This is achieved by adding IK constraints to certain bones.
8. **Setting Up Control Bones**: Control bones are not part of the actual skeleton but are used to control complex movements. For example, a control bone can be used to

control the entire hand or facial expressions.

9. **Creating Custom Bone Shapes**: Custom bone shapes can be created for easier selection and a clearer understanding of the rig. These are often used for facial rigs or complex mechanical rigs.
10. **Using Drivers for Advanced Rigging**: Drivers can be used to create relationships between different properties. For example, a driver might be used to make a character's eyes follow a target.
11. **Rigging for Facial Expressions**: Facial rigging can be complex, involving a combination of bones and shape keys. This allows for a wide range of expressions and lip sync.
12. **Using Constraints for Realistic Motion**: Constraints like 'Copy Rotation' or 'Limit Distance' can be used to restrict or guide the movement of bones for more realistic animations.
13. **Testing Your Rig**: It's important to test your rig by posing it in various positions to ensure the deformations look correct and the controls work as expected.
14. **Organizing Your Rig with Layers**: Armatures in Blender can be organized on different layers. This helps keep complex rigs manageable, allowing you to focus on specific parts of the rig.
15. **Locking and Hiding Bones**: For simplicity, you can lock the transformations of certain bones or hide them entirely. This prevents accidental modifications and keeps the rig tidy.
16. **Mirroring Bones for Symmetry**: For symmetrical characters, you can mirror bones across the central axis. This ensures uniformity in the rig.
17. **Rigging Non-Organic Objects**: Rigging isn't just for characters. Mechanical objects or creatures with non-

standard anatomy also require rigs, often involving more complex constraints and setups.

18. **Continuously Learning and Improving**: Rigging is a complex and nuanced aspect of 3D animation. Continuously learning new techniques and practicing on different types of models is key to improving your rigging skills.
19. **Collaborating with Animators**: If you're rigging for someone else, communication with the animator is crucial. Understanding their needs can help you create a more effective and animator-friendly rig.
20. **Utilizing Rigging Add-ons**: There are many add-ons available for Blender that can automate or simplify parts of the rigging process. These can be particularly useful for complex or repetitive tasks.

Rigging is an essential step in bringing your models to life through animation. A well-rigged model can be animated with greater ease and realism, making it a critical skill for any aspiring 3D animator.

5.3 Keyframe Animation and Motion Paths

Keyframe animation and motion paths are fundamental techniques in Blender that enable animators to create dynamic and fluid movements in their scenes. Understanding these concepts is essential for effective animation.

1. **What are Keyframes?**: Keyframes are points in time that define the start and end of any animation. They store the position, rotation, scale, or other properties of an object at a specific moment.
2. **Inserting Keyframes**: To insert a keyframe, position your object as desired, then press 'I' and select the property you

want to keyframe, such as location, rotation, or scale.

3. **Timeline and Keyframe Management**: The timeline at the bottom of the Blender interface shows your keyframes and allows you to manage them. You can move, copy, or delete keyframes as needed.
4. **Interpolation and Easing**: Between keyframes, Blender interpolates the values to create smooth motion. The type of interpolation, like linear or Bezier, can be adjusted for different easing effects.
5. **Graph Editor for Detailed Control**: The Graph Editor provides a detailed view of the animation curves. Here, you can fine-tune the interpolation and velocity of your animations.
6. **Animating with Auto Keyframe**: The Auto Keyframe mode allows you to automatically insert keyframes when you move, rotate, or scale an object, speeding up the animation process.
7. **Creating Motion Paths**: Motion paths visualize an object's trajectory over time. They can be enabled in the object properties panel, helping you to plan and adjust the movement more accurately.
8. **Editing Motion Paths**: Motion paths can be edited in the 3D view, allowing you to adjust the path directly for more intuitive control of your animation.
9. **Using the Dope Sheet for Overview**: The Dope Sheet gives an overview of all keyframes in your scene. It's useful for managing keyframes across multiple objects and actions.
10. **Blocking Out Animations**: Start by blocking out your animation with keyframes at major points of action. This rough pass helps establish timing and major movements before adding in-betweens.

11. **Layering Animations**: Animations can be layered by using multiple keyframes at different points, allowing for complex movements to be built up gradually.
12. **Non-Linear Animation (NLA) Editor**: For complex sequences, the NLA Editor allows you to blend and layer different actions, like walk cycles or gestures, in a non-destructive way.
13. **Animating Cameras and Lights**: Keyframe animation isn't just for objects and characters. Cameras and lights can also be animated to create dynamic scene changes.
14. **Using Constraints with Keyframes**: Constraints can be used in conjunction with keyframes to control the movement of objects, like making an object follow a path.
15. **Animating Material Properties**: You can animate almost any property in Blender, including material and texture settings, to create effects like changing colors, transparency, or emission.
16. **Understanding F-Curves**: F-Curves in the Graph Editor represent the relationship between time (frame number) and the value of a property. Adjusting these curves gives you precise control over the pacing and timing of your animation.
17. **Copying and Pasting Keyframes**: Keyframes can be copied and pasted, even between different objects. This is useful for creating repetitive actions or symmetrical movements.
18. **Using Markers for Synchronization**: Markers can be added to the timeline to mark important events or synchronization points in your animation.
19. **Previewing and Adjusting in Real-Time**: Utilize Blender's real-time playback to preview your animations and make adjustments on the fly for immediate feedback.

20. **Continuous Learning and Experimentation**: Animation is a skill that benefits greatly from continuous practice and experimentation. Try different techniques and challenges to develop your animation skills.

Keyframe animation and motion paths are powerful tools in Blender, providing the foundation for creating compelling and lifelike animations. By mastering these techniques, you can bring a new level of sophistication and expression to your 3D projects.

5.4 Advanced Animation Techniques: Lip Syncing and Facial Expressions

Creating realistic lip syncing and facial expressions is a challenging yet rewarding aspect of character animation in Blender. These advanced techniques add depth and emotion to characters, making them more lifelike and engaging.

1. **Understanding Facial Anatomy**: Knowing the basic anatomy of the face and how muscles work to create expressions is crucial for realistic animation. Study facial expressions and how the mouth moves during speech.
2. **Rigging for Facial Animation**: Create a detailed facial rig. This usually involves a combination of bones and shape keys (blend shapes) to control various parts of the face.
3. **Creating Shape Keys for Expressions**: Shape keys are used to deform the mesh for different expressions. Create a series of shape keys for common expressions like smiling, frowning, and eyebrow movements.
4. **Lip Syncing Basics**: For lip syncing, you need to break down speech into phonemes (basic units of sound). Each phoneme corresponds to a specific mouth shape.
5. **Animating Mouth Shapes**: Create keyframes for the

different mouth shapes that correspond to the phonemes in your audio track. Synchronize these keyframes with the audio for accurate lip syncing.

6. **Using Add-ons for Lip Syncing**: There are Blender add-ons available that can automate parts of the lip-syncing process by analyzing audio files and creating corresponding mouth movements.
7. **Facial Control Rigging**: Advanced rigs often include a facial control rig, which provides an intuitive interface for animating facial expressions. These can include sliders or facial UIs for easier animation.
8. **Combining Expressions and Lip Sync**: Combine lip movements with facial expressions for more dynamic and believable character animation. For example, incorporate eyebrow raises or squints along with speech.
9. **Animating Eyes and Eyelids**: The eyes play a significant role in conveying emotion. Animate the eyelids and eyeballs to match the mood and focus of the character.
10. **Fine-Tuning with the Graph Editor**: Use the Graph Editor to fine-tune the animation curves of your facial animations. Smooth transitions and proper easing are key for natural movement.
11. **Using Reference Videos**: Reference videos of people speaking or expressing emotions can be invaluable. Use them to study and replicate natural movements and timings.
12. **Layering Animations for Complexity**: Layer multiple animations for complexity. For example, animate the basic mouth movements first, then add detailed expressions and eye movements on top.
13. **Practicing Phoneme Shapes**: Spend time practicing animating the different phoneme shapes. Mastery of these

shapes is key to convincing lip-syncing.

14. **Timing and Spacing in Dialogue**: Pay attention to the timing and spacing of dialogue. Good pacing can make the difference between robotic and lifelike speech.
15. **Animating Breathing and Subtle Movements**: Don't forget to animate subtle movements like breathing or slight shifts in posture, which add life to your character even during dialogue.
16. **Performance Capture as a Reference**: If possible, use performance capture data as a reference for your animations. This can provide a realistic basis for your character's movements.
17. **Mimicking Real Speech Patterns**: Observe and mimic real speech patterns and idiosyncrasies. Everyone speaks differently, and capturing these nuances can add authenticity to your characters.
18. **Continuous Learning and Practice**: Facial animation and lip-syncing are skills that improve with practice. Continuously learn from each project and seek feedback to refine your techniques.
19. **Collaboration with Voice Actors**: If working with voice actors, collaboration can be key. Understanding their speech patterns and mannerisms can inform your animation decisions.
20. **Experimenting with Styles**: Depending on your project, experiment with different animation styles, from hyper-realistic to exaggerated or stylized, to match the tone and aesthetic of your work.

Mastering lip syncing and facial expressions in Blender is a journey that combines technical skill with artistic intuition. These advanced animation techniques are essential for bringing characters to life and connecting with the audience on an emotional level.

5.5 Utilizing Blender for Character Animation Projects

Character animation is a key aspect of many Blender projects, ranging from short films to video games. It involves bringing a character to life through movement and expression. Here's a guide to effectively using Blender for character animation.

1. **Concept and Character Design**: Before animating, it's important to have a well-designed character. Consider the character's personality, backstory, and physical attributes as these will influence its movements and expressions.
2. **Modeling the Character**: The character should be modeled with animation in mind. This means considering the range of motion and ensuring the topology is suitable for deformation.
3. **Rigging for Animation**: Rigging is the process of adding a skeleton and controls to your character. A good rig is essential for effective animation, allowing for natural and diverse movements.
4. **Creating Facial Rigs**: For expressive characters, a detailed facial rig is necessary. This often involves using bones or shape keys for different facial expressions and lip-syncing.
5. **Weight Painting for Deformations**: Proper weight painting ensures that the mesh deforms naturally with the rig. Pay special attention to joint areas like elbows, knees, and fingers.
6. **Animating with Keyframes**: Start animating your character using keyframes. Block out the main poses first,

then add in-between frames for smooth transitions.

7. **Using Reference Footage**: Reference footage can be invaluable for understanding movement dynamics and timing. Use videos of real people or animals as a guide for your animation.
8. **Principles of Animation**: Apply the 12 principles of animation such as anticipation, squash and stretch, and follow-through. These principles are crucial for creating believable and appealing motion.
9. **Working on Walk Cycles**: Walk cycles are a fundamental aspect of character animation. A realistic walk cycle requires attention to weight, balance, and the natural movement of limbs.
10. **Animating Expressions and Lip Sync**: For characters that speak or show emotion, animate the facial expressions and mouth movements to match dialogue and emotion.
11. **Non-Linear Animation (NLA) Editor**: For complex sequences, use the NLA Editor to blend and layer different actions, such as walking while talking or expressing emotions.
12. **Adding Secondary Motion**: Secondary motions, like hair or cloth movement, add realism to your character. Use Blender's physics systems or keyframe these elements for added dynamism.
13. **Character Interaction with Environment**: Ensure your character interacts believably with its environment, whether it's walking on uneven terrain or picking up objects.
14. **Camera Movement and Composition**: The camera's movement and composition play a big role in how the animation is perceived. Use camera angles and movements to enhance the storytelling.

15. **Lighting and Rendering for Animation**: Choose lighting and rendering settings that complement the character and scene. This can greatly affect the mood and visual appeal of the animation.
16. **Performance and Memory Considerations**: Character animation can be demanding on performance. Optimize your scene and use layers to manage complex animations.
17. **Feedback and Iteration**: Get feedback on your animations and be prepared to make adjustments. Animation often requires several iterations to get right.
18. **Using Add-ons and Tools**: Utilize Blender add-ons and tools designed for animation, which can streamline the animation process and add functionalities.
19. **Staying Organized**: Keep your project files, such as rigs, animations, and textures, well organized. This is especially important for larger projects with multiple characters and scenes.
20. **Continuous Learning and Experimentation**: Character animation is a field where there is always more to learn. Continuously practice, experiment with different styles and techniques, and stay updated with new Blender features and add-ons.

Character animation in Blender is a multi-faceted process that combines technical skill with creative storytelling. By mastering these aspects, you can create engaging and lifelike animations that resonate with audiences.

Chapter 6: Visual Effects and Simulation

Section 6.1: Creating Stunning Visual Effects in Blender

Visual effects (VFX) are an integral part of modern filmmaking and animation, and Blender offers a powerful toolkit for creating stunning VFX. In this section, we'll explore the various aspects of using Blender for VFX, from creating explosions to adding magical effects to your scenes.

6.1.1: Understanding VFX in Blender

Before diving into the technical details, it's essential to understand what VFX are and how they enhance storytelling. Visual effects encompass a wide range of techniques used to create or manipulate imagery in post-production or during live-action shooting. These effects can be anything from adding raindrops to simulating a full-blown alien invasion. Blender provides a comprehensive suite of tools to tackle these challenges.

6.1.2: Particle Systems and Simulations

One of the key features in Blender for creating VFX is its robust particle system. With it, you can simulate everything from rain and snow to fire and smoke. By adjusting parameters such as particle size, speed, and behavior, you can craft realistic-looking effects. Here's a basic example of creating a simple rain simulation in Blender:

```
# Blender Rain Simulation

import bpy

# Create a new particle system
```

```
particle_system = bpy.context.object.modifiers.new(name="Rain", type='PARTICLE')

particle_system.particle_system.settings.type = 'HAIR'

# Adjust settings for particle system

particle_system.particle_system.settings.hair_length = 1.0

particle_system.particle_system.settings.count = 1000

particle_system.particle_system.settings.subframes = 10

# Add turbulence to make the raindrops appear natural

turbulence = particle_system.particle_system.settings.force_fields.create(name="Turbule

turbulence.type = 'TURBULENCE'

turbulence.strength = 1.0

# Set up materials for raindrops

# (You can use a transparent material for raindrop objects)
```

6.1.3: Adding Explosive Effects

Blender's physics simulations allow you to create explosive effects like fiery explosions, debris, and destruction. You can use the Smoke and Fire simulation system to achieve this. Here's a simplified example of creating an explosion effect:

```
# Blender Explosion Simulation

import bpy

# Create an explosion simulation
```

```
bpy.ops.object.particle_system_add()

particle_system = bpy.context.object.particle_systems[0]

particle_system.settings.type = 'EXPLODE'

# Adjust explosion parameters

particle_system.settings.explosion_source = 'VERT'

particle_system.settings.explosion_source_group = bpy.data.objects['Debris'].vertex_groups.active

particle_system.settings.use_emit_random = False

particle_system.settings.frame_start = 1

particle_system.settings.frame_end = 30

# Set up materials for explosion debris
```

6.1.4: Magical Effects and Compositing

Blender's node-based compositor is a powerful tool for adding magical and other post-production effects to your scenes. You can combine different render passes, apply color grading, and add glows and flares to create enchanting visuals. Here's a basic example of adding a magical glow effect using the compositor:

```
# Blender Magical Glow Effect

import bpy

# Enable compositing

bpy.context.scene.use_nodes = True

tree = bpy.context.scene.node_tree
```

```
# Create a new Render Layer node

rl_node = tree.nodes.new(type='CompositorNodeRLayers')

rl_node.location = 0, 0

# Add a Glare node for glow effect

glare_node = tree.nodes.new(type='CompositorNodeGlare')

glare_node.location = 200, 0

glare_node.threshold = 0.5

glare_node.size = 10

# Connect nodes

tree.links.new(rl_node.outputs['Image'], glare_node.inputs[0])

tree.links.new(glare_node.outputs[0],
tree.nodes['Composite'].inputs['Image'])
```

These are just the tip of the iceberg when it comes to VFX in Blender. The software's flexibility, combined with your creativity, can lead to breathtaking visual effects that enhance your projects.

6.1.5: Resources and Further Learning

To delve deeper into Blender's VFX capabilities, consider exploring tutorials and courses specifically focused on VFX techniques. Websites like Blender Artists and Blender Stack Exchange are great places to seek advice and share your VFX creations with the Blender community. Additionally, the Blender Cloud offers high-quality training materials and assets related to VFX.

In this section, we've covered the fundamentals of creating stunning visual effects in Blender, from understanding the concept of VFX to utilizing particle systems, simulations, and compositing. Experiment with these techniques and let your imagination run wild to bring your visual effects to life in Blender.

Section 6.2: Simulating Physics: Fluid, Smoke, and Fire

Blender's physics simulations are a powerful tool for creating realistic fluid, smoke, and fire effects in your projects. In this section, we'll explore how to harness Blender's simulation capabilities to add dynamic and engaging elements to your scenes.

6.2.1: Fluid Simulation

Blender's fluid simulation system allows you to create realistic liquid effects, such as water flowing, splashing, and pouring. To get started with fluid simulation, you can follow these basic steps:

1. **Set Up the Domain:** Define the area in which the fluid will be simulated. This is known as the "domain." You can add a domain object and adjust its size and resolution.
2. **Create the Fluid Object:** Add a mesh object (e.g., a cube) and designate it as the fluid source. Adjust its settings to determine how the fluid will behave, such as whether it's an inflow (pouring water) or an obstacle (a container).
3. **Configure Simulation Settings:** Access the fluid simulation settings and specify the type of fluid (liquid, gas, or smoke) you want to simulate. Adjust parameters like viscosity, surface tension, and gravity to achieve the desired effect.
4. **Bake the Simulation:** Once you've set up the scene, you

need to bake the simulation. This process calculates the behavior of the fluid over time. The time it takes to bake depends on your computer's processing power and the complexity of the simulation.

5. **Render the Result:** After the simulation is baked, you can render the frames to create a fluid animation. Ensure you have suitable materials and lighting to make the fluid look realistic.

6.2.2: Smoke and Fire Simulation

Blender's smoke and fire simulation capabilities enable you to create realistic smoke plumes, fiery explosions, and more. Here's a simplified overview of creating a smoke simulation:

1. **Set Up the Domain:** Similar to fluid simulation, you need to create a domain object that defines the space in which smoke and fire will interact. Adjust the domain's size and resolution as needed.
2. **Add Emitters and Flow Objects:** Emitters are objects that emit smoke or fire. You can add objects like a cube or a sphere and designate them as emitters. Flow objects can control the direction and speed of the smoke or fire.
3. **Configure Simulation Settings:** Access the smoke and fire simulation settings to specify the type of effect you want. You can adjust parameters like temperature, combustion, and vorticity.
4. **Bake the Simulation:** Like fluid simulation, you'll need to bake the smoke and fire simulation. This step calculates how smoke and fire behave over time.
5. **Render the Result:** Once the simulation is baked, you can render the frames to create an animation of the smoke and fire. Consider using appropriate shaders and lighting to

make the effect realistic.

6.2.3: Combining Simulations

One of the strengths of Blender is its ability to combine multiple simulations. For example, you can create a scene where fluid interacts with fire, resulting in a realistic explosion with flames and smoke. To achieve this, you'll need to set up both fluid and fire simulations in the same scene and ensure they interact correctly.

6.2.4: Tips for Realistic Simulations

Creating realistic fluid, smoke, and fire simulations can be challenging, but here are some tips to enhance the realism of your effects:

- Pay attention to details such as texture and color for fluids, and adjust settings like turbulence and temperature for smoke and fire.

- Use reference images or videos to study real-world behavior and incorporate those insights into your simulations.

- Experiment with different resolution levels and simulation parameters to find the right balance between realism and computational resources.

- Combine simulations with other elements in your scene, such as lighting, materials, and compositing, to achieve a cohesive look.

In this section, we've explored the basics of simulating physics in Blender, specifically focusing on fluid, smoke, and fire effects.

Blender's simulation capabilities open up a world of possibilities for creating dynamic and engaging visuals in your projects. Experimentation and practice will help you master these powerful tools.

Section 6.3: Integrating Particle Systems for Dynamic Effects

Particle systems in Blender are versatile tools that allow you to create a wide range of dynamic effects, from realistic rain and snow to magical sparkles and explosions. In this section, we'll delve into the world of particle systems and explore how to integrate them into your Blender projects to add life and dynamism.

6.3.1: Understanding Particle Systems

Particle systems simulate the behavior of individual particles, which can represent anything from raindrops to dust to sparks. These particles can move, change color, and interact with each other and other objects in your scene. Blender offers two main types of particle systems: emitter particles and hair particles.

- **Emitter Particles:** Emitter particles originate from a mesh object and can be used to create effects like rain, fire, and smoke. You can adjust settings such as emission rate, lifetime, and initial velocity to control their behavior.

- **Hair Particles:** Hair particles are commonly used for creating fur, grass, and other natural phenomena. They consist of a series of connected particles that follow the contours of a mesh object. You can control the length, density, and randomness of hair particles.

6.3.2: Creating a Simple Particle System

Let's start by creating a basic particle system to simulate falling snow in Blender. Follow these steps:

1. **Add an Emitter Object:** Start by adding an object (e.g., a plane) that will serve as the emitter for the snow particles. Scale it to the desired size for your scene.
2. **Access Particle Settings:** Select the emitter object, go to the "Particle Properties" tab in the Properties Editor, and click "New" to create a new particle system.
3. **Configure Particle System:** In the particle settings, set the type to "Emitter." Adjust the following parameters to create the snowfall effect:

– **Emission:** Set the "Number" to control the density of snowflakes.

– **Velocity:** Adjust the initial velocity to make the snowflakes fall naturally.

– **Lifetime:** Set the lifetime to determine how long each snowflake stays visible.

– **Render:** Choose a snowflake-like object (e.g., a small plane with a snowflake texture) as the render object.

1. **Render the Scene:** To see the snowfall in your scene, go to the "Render" tab and click the "Render" button. You should now have a basic snowfall effect.

6.3.3: Advanced Particle Effects

Blender's particle systems offer extensive capabilities beyond simple effects. You can create complex interactions by combining multiple particle systems, controlling particles with force fields, and even scripting custom behaviors using Python.

For instance, you can simulate realistic fireworks by using multiple particle systems for different particle types (e.g., sparks, trails, and explosions) and using force fields to control their motion and behavior.

6.3.4: Particle Scripting

Blender allows you to script particle behavior using Python. This can be particularly useful for creating custom particle effects or complex interactions. Here's a basic example of Python code that creates a particle system and adds particles to it:

```
import bpy

# Create a new particle system

bpy.ops.object.particle_system_add()

particle_system = bpy.context.object.particle_systems[-1]

# Access the particle settings

settings = particle_system.settings

# Configure particle system properties

settings.type = 'EMITTER'

settings.count = 1000
```

```
settings.lifetime = 50

settings.emit_from = 'FACE'

settings.use_emit_random = True

settings.normal_factor = 0.5

# Set up materials and textures for the particles

# (You can assign materials and textures to the particle object)
```

6.3.5: Resources and Further Learning

To become proficient in using particle systems for dynamic effects in Blender, consider exploring tutorials, courses, and resources dedicated to particle simulations. Websites like Blender Stack Exchange and Blender Artists are excellent places to seek guidance and share your particle system creations with the Blender community.

In this section, we've explored the world of particle systems in Blender, from understanding their types to creating basic and advanced particle effects. Blender's particle capabilities offer endless creative possibilities for adding dynamic and lifelike elements to your 3D projects. Experimentation and practice will help you master the art of particle simulations.

Section 6.4: Crafting Realistic Environments with Environmental Effects

Creating realistic environments in Blender is not just about modeling and texturing; it's also about adding environmental effects that breathe life into your scenes. In this section, we'll explore how to craft realistic environments by incorporating various environmental effects and techniques.

6.4.1: Understanding Environmental Effects

Environmental effects in Blender can transform a static scene into a dynamic and immersive world. These effects include things like fog, rain, mist, and sunlight. When used effectively, they can significantly enhance the realism and atmosphere of your 3D environments.

6.4.2: Adding Atmospheric Effects

One common environmental effect is atmospheric perspective, which simulates how distant objects appear fainter and bluer due to the scattering of light in the atmosphere. To create atmospheric perspective in Blender, you can use the following techniques:

- **Depth of Field (DOF):** Blender's camera settings allow you to enable DOF, which blurs objects that are not in focus. This simulates the effect of distant objects appearing slightly hazy.

- **Color Grading:** Adjusting the colors in your scene can mimic the bluish and desaturated appearance of distant objects. Use the Compositor in Blender to apply color grading effects.

- **Mist Pass:** Blender provides a Mist Pass that can be used to control the intensity of atmospheric effects based on distance from the camera. You can add this pass to your render layers and adjust its settings.

6.4.3: Simulating Weather and Precipitation

To create realistic rain, snow, or other forms of precipitation in Blender, you can use particle systems and shaders:

- **Rain:** Set up an emitter object (e.g., a plane) to emit raindrops as particles. Adjust the particle settings to control their size, speed, and lifespan. Use a raindrop texture and material to make them appear realistic.

- **Snow:** Create a similar setup as with rain but use different particle settings and materials to mimic snowflakes. Adjust the speed and size of the particles to achieve a convincing snowfall effect.

6.4.4: Utilizing Lighting for Realism

Lighting plays a crucial role in creating realistic environments. Consider the following techniques:

- **HDRI (High Dynamic Range Imaging):** HDRI lighting provides realistic outdoor lighting by using high-resolution images of real-world environments. You can use HDRI images as environmental maps to light your scenes accurately.

- **Sunlight and Sky:** Blender's Cycles renderer features a "Sun Lamp" that mimics natural sunlight. Position the Sun Lamp to match the direction and angle of the sun in your scene. You can also use a "Sky Texture" node in the Shader Editor to create a realistic sky background.

6.4.5: Integrating Environmental Audio

Realism in environments isn't limited to visuals. Sound can enhance the immersive experience. Blender supports audio integration, so you can add ambient sounds like wind, rain, or birdsong to your scenes. You can import audio files and sync them with your animations to create a more immersive environment.

6.4.6: Performance Considerations

While adding environmental effects is essential for realism, it's crucial to optimize your scenes for performance, especially if you're working on real-time projects or animations. Consider using techniques like level of detail (LOD) models and optimizing particle systems to maintain smooth performance without sacrificing realism.

In conclusion, crafting realistic environments in Blender involves more than just modeling and texturing. It requires an understanding of environmental effects, lighting, atmospheric perspective, and audio integration. These elements come together to create immersive and believable 3D worlds. Experiment with these techniques to elevate the quality of your Blender projects and captivate your audience with realistic environments.

Section 6.5: Tips for Combining CGI with Live-Action Footage

Combining computer-generated imagery (CGI) with live-action footage is a common practice in filmmaking, and Blender provides powerful tools to seamlessly integrate these elements. In this section, we'll explore tips and techniques for achieving a convincing blend between CGI and live-action footage in your projects.

6.5.1: Match Lighting and Camera Settings

One of the most critical aspects of integrating CGI with live-action footage is ensuring that the lighting and camera settings match. Here's how to achieve this:

- **Reference Footage:** Use the live-action footage as a reference for lighting and camera angles. Analyze the lighting conditions, shadows, and camera perspectives in the footage.

- **Environment Maps:** Employ environment maps or HDRIs (High Dynamic Range Images) to match the lighting. Blender allows you to use these images as lighting sources to replicate the real-world lighting in your CGI elements.

- **Camera Tracking:** If the live-action footage features camera movement, perform camera tracking using Blender's built-in camera tracking tools. This will enable your CGI elements to move realistically with the live-action scene.

6.5.2: Use Green Screens and Keying

When shooting live-action footage with the intention of compositing CGI elements, consider using green screens or blue screens for easy background removal (keying). Here's a simple workflow:

- **Shoot on a Green Screen:** Record your live-action footage with the subject(s) against a green or blue screen background.

- **Keying in Blender:** In Blender's Video Sequence Editor (VSE), you can use the "Keying" node to remove the green or blue background and replace it with your CGI elements. Adjust the settings to fine-tune the keying process.

- **Match Lighting:** Ensure that the lighting on your CGI elements matches the lighting conditions of the live-action scene, considering factors like shadows and reflections.

6.5.3: Compositing and Layering

Blender offers a powerful compositing system that allows you to combine multiple layers of footage, including live-action and CGI elements. Here are some compositing tips:

- **Use Layers:** Organize your CGI and live-action elements on separate layers within Blender's Compositor. This allows you to apply effects and adjustments independently.

- **Depth Pass:** Utilize a depth pass or depth map to create realistic depth of field effects and post-process blur on your CGI elements to match the live-action footage.

- **Color Correction:** Apply color correction and grading to both the live-action and CGI elements to achieve a consistent and cohesive look. Blender's Compositor provides nodes for these adjustments.

6.5.4: Motion Blur and Integration

Motion blur is essential for achieving a natural integration between CGI and live-action elements, especially when there's camera movement. Here's how to work with motion blur:

- **Enable Motion Blur:** Ensure motion blur is enabled for your CGI objects. In Blender's render settings, you can adjust the motion blur settings to match the motion in your live-action footage.

- **Shadows and Reflections:** Pay attention to how shadows and reflections interact between the CGI and live-action elements. Properly matching these elements can make the integration more convincing.

6.5.5: Fine-Tune and Test

Achieving a seamless blend between CGI and live-action footage often requires fine-tuning and testing. Here's a workflow to consider:

- **Test Shots:** Perform test shots or render test frames to assess the integration. This helps identify any issues early in the process.

- **Iterate:** Don't hesitate to iterate and make adjustments. This may involve refining keying, tweaking lighting, or making subtle changes to the CGI elements.

- **Feedback:** Seek feedback from others, especially if you have access to a team or colleagues. Fresh perspectives can help identify areas for improvement.

In conclusion, combining CGI with live-action footage is a complex but rewarding process in Blender. By matching lighting and camera settings, using green screens for keying, effective compositing and layering, applying motion blur, and fine-tuning your work, you can achieve convincing integration that enhances the storytelling in your projects. Blender's versatility and compositing tools make it a valuable resource for filmmakers and visual effects artists.

Chapter 7: Blender in Game Development

Section 7.1: Blender's Role in the Game Development Pipeline

Blender has become an indispensable tool in the world of game development, playing a vital role in various stages of the game creation pipeline. In this section, we'll explore Blender's significance in game development and how it contributes to different aspects of the process.

7.1.1: Asset Creation

Blender excels in asset creation for games. Game assets include 3D models, textures, animations, and more. Blender's powerful modeling capabilities allow game artists to create characters, props, and environments. The ability to UV unwrap and texture these models directly within Blender streamlines the workflow. Furthermore, Blender supports a wide range of file formats used in game engines, ensuring compatibility with popular game development platforms like Unity and Unreal Engine.

7.1.2: Character Modeling and Rigging

Character modeling and rigging are crucial components of game development, and Blender offers robust solutions for both. Artists can create intricate character models using Blender's sculpting and modeling tools. The character rigging system allows for the creation of skeletons and bones, enabling realistic animations and interactions. Blender's Weight Paint mode simplifies the process of assigning weights to bones, facilitating smooth character movement.

7.1.3: Animation

Blender's animation capabilities extend to game development, enabling the creation of lifelike character movements and object animations. Artists can utilize keyframe animation, armature-based animation, and shape keys to craft dynamic sequences. Blender also supports the export of animations in formats compatible with game engines, ensuring seamless integration into game projects.

7.1.4: Level Design

Blender is a versatile tool for level design in game development. Game designers can construct intricate game environments and landscapes, taking advantage of Blender's modeling and sculpting tools. The ability to import real-world heightmaps and satellite imagery simplifies the creation of detailed terrains. Additionally, Blender's real-time rendering engines like Eevee allow designers to visualize and iterate on level designs efficiently.

7.1.5: Texture Painting

Texture painting is a critical aspect of game asset creation, and Blender offers a dedicated Texture Paint mode for this purpose. Artists can paint directly onto 3D models, adding intricate details, colors, and textures. Blender also supports the use of external image editors for more advanced texture painting workflows.

7.1.6: Physics Simulations

Blender's physics simulations are valuable for game development, particularly for creating realistic interactive experiences. Artists can simulate physics-based interactions such as fluid dynamics, cloth simulations, and rigid body dynamics within Blender. These simulations can be exported to game engines to enhance gameplay realism.

7.1.7: Prototyping and Previsualization

Before full-scale game development begins, prototyping and previsualization are essential stages in the game creation process. Blender's rapid modeling and animation capabilities make it an ideal tool for quickly visualizing game concepts. Game designers can create prototypes, mock-ups, and storyboards to test ideas and refine gameplay mechanics.

7.1.8: Exporting to Game Engines

Blender supports various export formats commonly used in game engines. Game developers can seamlessly transfer 3D models, animations, and textures from Blender to engines like Unity and Unreal Engine. This compatibility streamlines the integration of assets and ensures that the final game closely matches the original design.

In summary, Blender's role in game development is multifaceted and critical. It serves as a comprehensive tool for asset creation, character modeling, rigging, animation, level design, texture painting, physics simulations, prototyping, and exporting to game engines. Its versatility and feature set make it a preferred choice for game artists and developers looking to create engaging and immersive gaming experiences. Blender's integration with popular game engines solidifies its position as a vital asset in the game development pipeline.

Section 7.2: Creating Game Assets in Blender

Blender is a versatile and powerful tool for creating game assets, including 3D models, textures, animations, and more. In this section, we'll explore the process of creating game assets in Blender and how it fits into the game development workflow.

7.2.1: 3D Modeling for Games

Blender's modeling capabilities are at the core of game asset creation. Whether you're designing characters, props, or environments, Blender's modeling tools provide the flexibility needed to bring your game ideas to life.

- **Low-Poly Modeling:** Game assets often require low-poly models to optimize performance in real-time environments. Blender allows you to create efficient low-poly models while maintaining visual quality.

- **High-Poly Modeling:** For detailed assets that don't need to be real-time, Blender's sculpting tools come in handy. You can create high-poly models with intricate details and then generate low-poly versions for use in the game engine.

7.2.2: UV Mapping and Texturing

Texturing is a critical aspect of game asset creation, and Blender simplifies the process with its UV mapping tools:

- **UV Unwrapping:** Blender's UV unwrapping tools help you create a 2D representation (UV map) of your 3D model. This map is essential for applying textures accurately.

- **Texture Painting:** Blender's Texture Paint mode allows you to paint directly onto 3D models, adding color, detail, and texture. This is particularly useful for creating character skins, environment textures, and more.

7.2.3: Animation and Rigging

For game characters and objects that require movement, Blender's animation and rigging tools are invaluable:

- **Character Rigging:** Blender's armature system enables you to create skeletons for characters, making them poseable and ready for animation. You can also use Blender's automatic weights or weight painting tools to assign bone influences to mesh vertices.

- **Keyframe Animation:** Blender supports keyframe animation, allowing you to create lifelike character movements and object animations. The animation timeline and graph editor provide precise control over animations.

7.2.4: Exporting to Game Engines

Blender offers various export options to transfer your game assets to popular game engines like Unity, Unreal Engine, and Godot:

- **FBX Format:** The FBX format is widely supported by game engines and is an excellent choice for exporting 3D models, animations, and rigs from Blender.

- **Collada (DAE) Format:** Collada is another format commonly used for asset exchange between Blender and game engines. It supports animations and is suitable for exporting complex scenes.

- **Textures and Materials:** Blender allows you to export textures and materials along with 3D models, ensuring that your assets retain their visual quality in the game engine.

7.2.5: Optimization and LODs

To ensure optimal game performance, it's essential to optimize your assets. Blender provides tools and techniques for optimization:

- **Decimation Modifier:** The Decimation modifier in Blender allows you to reduce the polygon count of models while preserving their shape. This is useful for creating LODs (Level of Detail) for distant objects.

- **Texture Compression:** Blender supports texture compression formats commonly used in game engines. Compressing textures reduces memory usage and loading times.

7.2.6: Prototyping and Iteration

Blender is also an excellent tool for prototyping game assets. Game developers and artists can quickly create rough versions of characters, environments, or props to test gameplay mechanics and visual concepts. The iterative nature of Blender allows for continuous refinement until the desired results are achieved.

In conclusion, Blender plays a significant role in the game development pipeline by serving as a comprehensive tool for creating game assets. Whether you're designing 3D models, texturing, animating, or preparing assets for export to game engines, Blender's versatility and feature set make it an invaluable asset for game artists and developers. Its integration with popular game engines ensures a seamless transition from asset creation to game development.

Section 7.3: Optimizing Models for Real-Time Rendering

Optimizing 3D models for real-time rendering is a critical step in game development. Blender provides a range of tools and techniques to ensure that your models run smoothly in game engines without sacrificing visual quality. In this section, we'll explore how to optimize 3D models in Blender for real-time rendering.

7.3.1: Reduce Polygon Count

One of the primary considerations for real-time rendering is to reduce the polygon count of your 3D models. Lower-poly models are essential for maintaining smooth performance. Blender offers several methods to achieve this:

- **Decimation Modifier:** The Decimation modifier simplifies models by reducing the number of polygons while preserving shape. Adjust the ratio parameter to control the level of simplification.

- **Manual Retopology:** For more control, you can manually retopologize models by creating a new, lower-poly mesh over the existing high-poly model. Blender's Retopology tools, like the Snap to Face feature, assist in this process.

7.3.2: Use LODs (Level of Detail)

Implementing Level of Detail (LOD) models is a common practice in game development. LODs provide different versions of a model with varying polygon counts, depending on the distance from the camera. Blender supports LOD creation:

- **Create LOD Models:** Duplicate your model and simplify each copy to create LODs with decreasing polygon counts. Name them accordingly (e.g., "High," "Medium," "Low").

- **Import LODs in Game Engine:** Game engines like Unity and Unreal Engine have built-in LOD systems that automatically switch between LOD models based on the camera's distance from the object.

7.3.3: Texture Optimization

Optimizing textures is crucial for efficient real-time rendering. Large texture sizes can consume significant memory and impact performance. Consider these texture optimization techniques:

- **Texture Compression:** Use texture compression formats supported by game engines, such as DXT (DDS) or ASTC. Blender allows you to export textures in these formats.

- **Texture Atlases:** Combine multiple textures into a single texture atlas. This reduces the number of texture calls and improves rendering efficiency.

- **Texture Resolution:** Adjust the resolution of textures to match the level of detail required. Lower resolution textures can be used for distant objects.

7.3.4: Remove Unnecessary Geometry

Clean up your 3D models by removing unnecessary geometry and hidden faces:

- **Delete Hidden Faces:** In Edit mode, select and delete faces that are not visible from the camera's perspective. These hidden faces can contribute to unnecessary rendering overhead.

- **Remove Doubles:** Blender provides a "Remove Doubles" function to merge overlapping vertices, reducing the vertex count.

7.3.5: Bake Normal Maps and Ambient Occlusion

To maintain the appearance of high-poly models while using low-poly versions, consider baking normal maps and ambient occlusion maps:

- **Normal Maps:** Bake normal maps from high-poly models to apply detailed surface information to low-poly versions. This creates the illusion of additional geometry.

- **Ambient Occlusion Maps:** Ambient occlusion maps add shading details to models, enhancing their realism.

Bake ambient occlusion maps to save computational resources.

7.3.6: Use Efficient Shaders

Shader complexity can impact real-time rendering performance. To optimize shaders in Blender:

- **Simplify Shaders:** Streamline your shaders by removing unnecessary nodes and complex calculations. Use simpler shaders when appropriate.

- **Shader LODs:** Implement shader LODs, similar to model LODs, to switch between different shader complexity levels based on distance.

7.3.7: Test and Profile

Optimization is an iterative process. Regularly test your models in the target game engine to profile their performance. Game engines often provide profiling tools that help identify performance bottlenecks. Make adjustments as needed to ensure a smooth gameplay experience.

In summary, optimizing 3D models for real-time rendering is crucial for game development. Blender offers a range of tools and techniques, including reducing polygon counts, implementing LODs, optimizing textures, cleaning up geometry, baking maps, using efficient shaders, and testing and profiling. By following these guidelines, you can strike a balance between visual quality and performance, ensuring that your game runs smoothly on a variety of hardware configurations.

Section 7.4: Exporting Assets for Game

Engines

Once you've created and optimized your game assets in Blender, the next crucial step is exporting them for use in game engines like Unity, Unreal Engine, or Godot. In this section, we'll explore the process of exporting assets from Blender, ensuring compatibility and a seamless integration into your chosen game engine.

7.4.1: Supported Export Formats

Blender supports various export formats commonly used in game development. These formats ensure that your 3D models, animations, textures, and other assets can be readily imported into your game engine of choice. Some of the supported formats include:

- **FBX (Filmbox):** FBX is a widely adopted format that is compatible with most game engines. It supports 3D models, animations, materials, and more. Blender's FBX exporter offers options for fine-tuning export settings.

- **Collada (DAE):** Collada is another common format used for asset exchange. It supports animations, materials, and hierarchy information. Blender's Collada exporter provides a straightforward way to export models in this format.

- **GLTF (GL Transmission Format):** GLTF is gaining popularity as a lightweight and efficient format for web and real-time applications. Blender has a dedicated GLTF exporter that simplifies the export process.

- **OBJ (Wavefront):** OBJ is a straightforward format that can be used for exporting 3D models. While it doesn't support animations, it's suitable for static objects.

Ensure that you choose the format that is best supported by your game engine and suits your project's requirements.

7.4.2: Exporting Meshes

When exporting 3D models, it's essential to consider mesh settings to ensure a smooth transition to the game engine:

- **Apply Scale and Rotation:** Before exporting, apply scale and rotation to your mesh. This ensures that the mesh maintains its orientation and size in the game engine.

- **Normals and Double-Sided Faces:** Verify that normals are correctly oriented and that there are no double-sided faces, as these can cause rendering issues.

- **UV Maps and Materials:** Ensure that UV maps and materials are correctly assigned to the mesh. The game engine relies on UV maps for texture mapping and materials for shading.

7.4.3: Exporting Animations

If your project involves character animations or object animations, exporting them correctly is crucial:

- **Keyframe Animation:** For keyframe animations, make sure you've baked the animations and that they are correctly framed and timed in your Blender project.

- **Armature Animation:** When exporting armature-based animations, ensure that the armature is correctly bound to the mesh and that animations are correctly rigged and weighted.

- **Export Options:** Most export formats, like FBX, Collada, and GLTF, offer specific options for exporting animations. Review these options to ensure that your animations are exported correctly.

7.4.4: Texture and Material Export

Textures and materials play a significant role in the visual quality of your game assets. When exporting textures and materials:

- **Texture Paths:** Ensure that texture paths are correctly set and that textures are in accessible locations relative to the exported asset. Some game engines allow you to automatically import textures along with the asset.

- **Material Compatibility:** Check that the materials used in Blender are compatible with the shader systems of your chosen game engine. You may need to make adjustments in the game engine to achieve the desired look.

7.4.5: Exporting Lights and Cameras

If your Blender project includes lights and cameras, exporting them can be essential for maintaining scene integrity:

- **Lights:** Exported lights can be useful for replicating specific lighting setups in the game engine. Ensure that the exported light settings match your desired in-game lighting.

- **Cameras:** Exporting cameras is essential if you have specific camera angles or shots that you want to reproduce in the game engine. Verify that camera settings, including field of view and clipping distances, are correctly configured.

7.4.6: Importing and Testing in the Game Engine

Once you've exported your assets from Blender, import them into your game engine. Each engine has its import process, but common steps include specifying import options, setting up materials and shaders, and assigning animations to characters or objects.

Testing your assets within the game engine is crucial. Ensure that textures, animations, and shaders are working as intended. Address any issues or discrepancies between Blender and the game engine, making the necessary adjustments.

In summary, exporting assets from Blender for game engines is a vital step in the game development pipeline. Understanding the supported export formats, optimizing your meshes, correctly exporting animations, managing textures and materials, and importing and testing in the game engine are all critical aspects of this process. Properly exporting assets ensures that your game development project maintains consistency and visual quality while benefiting from the capabilities of your chosen game engine.

Section 7.5: Collaborating with Game Developers as a Blender Artist

Collaboration between Blender artists and game developers is crucial for the successful execution of game projects. Game development is a multidisciplinary endeavor, and effective communication and collaboration are key to bringing creative visions to life. In this section, we'll explore how Blender artists can collaborate seamlessly with game developers.

7.5.1: Understanding Game Development Concepts

As a Blender artist collaborating with game developers, it's essential to have a basic understanding of game development concepts. Familiarize yourself with terms like assets, levels, character controllers, and game engines. This knowledge will facilitate communication and help you align your work with the technical requirements of the game project.

7.5.2: Communication and Planning

Clear communication and effective planning are the cornerstones of successful collaboration. Here are some strategies for fostering collaboration:

- **Project Briefs:** Work closely with game developers to understand project goals and requirements. Document project briefs that outline asset specifications, including polygon budgets, texture sizes, and animation needs.

- **Regular Meetings:** Schedule regular meetings or check-ins with the development team. These meetings provide opportunities to discuss progress, address questions, and make necessary adjustments.

- **Version Control:** Utilize version control systems like Git or SVN to manage and track changes to assets. This ensures that everyone is working with the latest versions and helps avoid conflicts.

7.5.3: Asset Integration

Game developers often work with various asset management tools and game engines. Ensure that your Blender assets can be seamlessly integrated into these workflows:

- **Asset Naming Conventions:** Follow naming conventions that are consistent with the game engine's requirements. Well-structured names make asset management more accessible.

- **Export Settings:** Tailor your export settings to match the game engine's import requirements. Verify the compatibility of formats, scale, and coordinate systems.

7.5.4: Asset Optimization

Optimizing assets for real-time rendering in game engines is a shared responsibility between Blender artists and developers:

- **Polygon Count:** Respect the agreed-upon polygon budgets for assets. Minimize unnecessary geometry to ensure optimal performance.

- **Texture Compression:** Export textures in formats compatible with the game engine and utilize texture compression for efficiency.

- **LODs:** Collaborate with developers to implement Level of Detail (LOD) models to improve rendering performance at various distances.

7.5.5: Feedback and Iteration

Expect and welcome feedback from game developers. The iterative process is common in game development, and adjustments may be needed:

- **Feedback Loop:** Create a feedback loop with the development team to review and iterate on assets. Address comments and concerns promptly.

- **Prototyping:** Be prepared for prototyping phases where assets may undergo rapid changes as the gameplay mechanics are refined.

7.5.6: Asset Delivery and Documentation

When delivering assets to game developers, consider the following:

- **Asset Packaging:** Organize assets systematically in project folders, including textures, materials, and models. Include any necessary files or documentation.

- **Documentation:** Provide clear documentation on asset usage, including material setup, animation instructions, and any special considerations.

7.5.7: Collaboration Tools

Leverage collaboration tools to streamline communication and asset sharing:

- **Project Management Software:** Use project management tools like Trello, Asana, or Jira to track tasks, milestones, and deadlines.

- **File Sharing and Cloud Services:** Utilize cloud-based storage solutions like Dropbox, Google Drive, or OneDrive for sharing and collaborating on assets.

- **Communication Platforms:** Choose communication platforms such as Slack, Discord, or Microsoft Teams for real-time discussions and updates.

7.5.8: Adaptability and Flexibility

Finally, be adaptable and flexible in your collaboration efforts. Game development is dynamic, and requirements may change. Your willingness to adjust and accommodate evolving project needs will be appreciated by the development team.

In conclusion, collaborating with game developers as a Blender artist is a collaborative process that involves effective communication, planning, and adherence to game development standards. By understanding game development concepts, optimizing assets, providing clear documentation, and leveraging collaboration tools, you can contribute to the successful creation of immersive and engaging games. Collaboration between artists and developers is essential for bringing creative visions to life in the world of game development.

Chapter 8: Scripting and Automation

Section 8.1: Introduction to Python Scripting in Blender

Python scripting is a powerful tool in Blender that allows you to automate tasks, create custom tools, and extend Blender's functionality. In this section, we'll introduce you to Python scripting in Blender, covering the basics and providing insights into how you can harness the power of scripting to enhance your workflow.

8.1.1: Python in Blender

Blender uses Python as its scripting language, making it accessible to both 3D artists and programmers. Python is known for its readability and versatility, making it an ideal choice for scripting tasks in Blender.

You can access Python scripting in Blender through the "Scripting" workspace, where you'll find the Text Editor and Python Console. The Text Editor allows you to write and execute scripts, while the Python Console provides an interactive environment for testing and debugging Python code.

8.1.2: Scripting Basics

To get started with Python scripting in Blender, you'll need to understand some fundamental concepts:

- **Syntax:** Python has a straightforward and human-readable syntax. It uses indentation (whitespace) to define code blocks, making it easy to read and write.

- **Variables:** You can use variables to store data, such as numbers, text, or objects. Variables in Python are dynamically typed, meaning their type can change during runtime.

- **Operators:** Python supports various operators for performing mathematical and logical operations. These include +, -, *, /, and logical operators like and, or, and not.

- **Functions:** Functions are reusable blocks of code that can be called with specific arguments. Blender provides a rich set of functions and modules for 3D tasks.

8.1.3: Blender's Python API

Blender's Python API (Application Programming Interface) exposes Blender's functionality to Python scripts. You can use the API to interact with objects, scenes, materials, and more. The API provides access to a vast array of functions and properties that allow you to manipulate Blender's data and perform various tasks.

To access the API, you can use the "bpy" module, which stands for Blender Python. This module contains submodules for different aspects of Blender, such as bpy.data for accessing data like meshes and materials, bpy.context for the current context in Blender, and bpy.ops for operators that perform actions in Blender.

8.1.4: Writing Your First Script

Let's create a simple script to get a feel for Python scripting in Blender. Open the Text Editor in Blender's Scripting workspace, create a new text block, and enter the following code:

```
import bpy

# Get the active object

active_object = bpy.context.active_object

# Print the object's name

print("Active Object:", active_object.name)
```

This script imports the bpy module, retrieves the active object, and prints its name to the console. To run the script, click the "Run

Script" button in the Text Editor. You should see the name of the active object displayed in the Python Console.

8.1.5: Automation and Customization

One of the significant advantages of Python scripting in Blender is automation. You can automate repetitive tasks by scripting them, saving you time and reducing the chance of errors.

Additionally, Python scripting allows you to create custom tools and add-ons tailored to your specific needs. You can design custom user interfaces, automate complex operations, and extend Blender's functionality beyond its default capabilities.

8.1.6: Learning Resources

To become proficient in Python scripting for Blender, consider exploring the following resources:

- Blender's official documentation provides comprehensive information on Blender's Python API and scripting capabilities.

- Online tutorials and courses specifically focused on Python scripting in Blender can help you build your skills and knowledge.

- Community forums and Blender's active developer community can be valuable sources of guidance and support when you encounter scripting challenges.

In conclusion, Python scripting in Blender opens up a world of possibilities for automation, customization, and extending Blender's capabilities. This introduction provides a foundation for further exploration and development of your scripting skills within the

Blender environment. Whether you're a 3D artist looking to streamline your workflow or a developer seeking to enhance Blender's functionality, Python scripting is a valuable tool to master.

Section 8.2: Automating Tasks with Custom Scripts

One of the primary benefits of Python scripting in Blender is the ability to automate repetitive tasks and create custom scripts that simplify complex operations. In this section, we'll delve into the world of automation with Blender's Python scripting, exploring how to create custom scripts to streamline your workflow and save time.

8.2.1: Identifying Repetitive Tasks

Before you start writing custom scripts, it's essential to identify the repetitive tasks in your workflow that can benefit from automation. These tasks can range from simple operations like renaming objects to more complex processes like setting up scene lighting or materials.

For example, imagine you frequently import a specific model format and apply the same scale and rotation corrections. Instead of performing these steps manually each time, you can create a script to automate the entire process.

8.2.2: Writing Custom Scripts

To write custom scripts in Blender, you can use the Text Editor in the Scripting workspace. Here's a simple example of a script that renames all selected objects by adding a prefix:

```
import bpy

# Get the selected objects
```

```
selected_objects = bpy.context.selected_objects

# Define a prefix

prefix = "New_"

# Rename selected objects

for obj in selected_objects:

obj.name = prefix + obj.name
```

In this script, we import the bpy module, retrieve the selected objects, and define a prefix. Then, we loop through the selected objects and rename each by adding the prefix. After writing the script, click the "Run Script" button to execute it.

8.2.3: Using Operators

Blender provides a wide range of operators that perform various actions. You can access these operators through scripting to automate tasks. For example, to add a cube to the scene using a script, you can use the bpy.ops.mesh.primitive_cube_add() operator:

```
import bpy

# Add a cube to the scene

bpy.ops.mesh.primitive_cube_add(size=2, enter_editmode=False, align='WORLD', location=(0, 0, 0))
```

This script adds a cube to the scene with specific parameters, such as size and location.

8.2.4: Automating Scene Setup

Python scripting is particularly useful for automating scene setup. For instance, if you often work with specific render settings or lighting setups, you can create scripts to apply them instantly.

Here's an example of a script that sets up basic lighting for a scene:

```
import bpy

# Add a point light

bpy.ops.object.light_add(type='POINT', align='WORLD', location=(0, 0, 5))

# Configure light settings

light = bpy.context.object

light.data.energy = 1000

light.data.specular_factor = 2
```

This script adds a point light to the scene, positions it, and configures its energy and specular factor.

8.2.5: Creating Custom Add-ons

For more extensive functionality and user-friendly interfaces, you can create custom add-ons in Blender. Add-ons are collections of Python scripts bundled together with user interface elements, making them accessible through Blender's interface.

Creating a complete add-on goes beyond the scope of this section, but Blender's official documentation provides detailed guides on developing add-ons. You can create add-ons to automate specific tasks, extend Blender's functionality, or enhance your workflow.

8.2.6: Sharing and Reusing Scripts

Python scripts in Blender are shareable and reusable. You can save your scripts as .py files and share them with others or use them across different projects. Sharing your scripts with the Blender community can also be a way to contribute to the community and receive feedback and improvements from others.

8.2.7: Debugging and Error Handling

As you write more complex scripts, you may encounter errors or unexpected behavior. Blender's Python environment includes debugging tools, and you can use print statements to output information for troubleshooting. Additionally, learning to handle errors gracefully with try-except blocks can make your scripts more robust.

8.2.8: Learning Resources

To become proficient in automating tasks with custom scripts in Blender, consider exploring the following learning resources:

- Blender's official documentation provides extensive information on scripting, including tutorials and reference materials.

- Online Python scripting tutorials and courses tailored to Blender can help you deepen your scripting skills.

- Blender Stack Exchange and Blender Artists forums are excellent places to ask questions, seek help, and share your scripts with the Blender community.

In conclusion, Python scripting in Blender offers endless possibilities for automating tasks, creating custom tools, and enhancing your workflow. By identifying repetitive tasks, writing custom scripts, and exploring Blender's Python API and operators, you can significantly increase your productivity and efficiency as a 3D artist or developer. Custom scripts and add-ons empower you to tailor Blender to your specific needs and streamline your creative process.

Section 8.3: Creating Add-ons and Plugins

Creating add-ons and plugins is a powerful way to extend Blender's functionality and tailor it to your specific needs. In this section, we'll explore the process of developing add-ons and plugins in Blender, providing you with the knowledge and tools to enhance your 3D workflow.

8.3.1: Understanding Add-ons and Plugins

In Blender, the terms "add-ons" and "plugins" are often used interchangeably. They refer to custom scripts or packages of scripts that provide new features, tools, or capabilities within Blender. Add-ons can be as simple as a single script or as complex as a collection of scripts, user interfaces, and integrated tools.

Add-ons are designed to extend Blender's functionality, and they can cover a wide range of areas, from modeling and texturing to rendering and animation. Whether you want to automate a specific task, streamline your workflow, or introduce entirely new features, creating an add-on is the way to go.

8.3.2: Developing Your First Add-on

Creating a custom add-on in Blender typically involves the following steps:

1. **Script Development:** Write Python scripts that define the

functionality you want to add to Blender. These scripts can include operators, panels, menus, and more.

2. **Registering and Unregistering:** In your scripts, you'll use Blender's Python API to register and unregister your add-on. Registration makes your add-on available for use in Blender, while unregistering removes it when necessary.
3. **User Interface (UI):** You can create custom user interfaces for your add-on, making it user-friendly and accessible through Blender's interface.
4. **Documentation:** Provide clear documentation that explains how to use your add-on, its purpose, and any specific instructions for users.
5. **Testing:** Thoroughly test your add-on to ensure it works correctly and doesn't cause errors or crashes in Blender.

8.3.3: Structure of an Add-on

A typical add-on in Blender consists of several components:

- **Python Scripts:** These scripts define the functionality of your add-on. They may include operators, properties, and handlers.

- **User Interface (UI):** If your add-on requires a user interface, you can create panels, menus, buttons, and other elements to interact with your add-on.

- **Registration and Unregistration:** You'll use the register() and unregister() functions to make your add-on available when enabled and remove it when disabled.

- **Documentation:** Clear documentation, often provided as comments within the code or in separate files, helps users understand how to use your add-on effectively.

8.3.4: An Example Add-on

Let's take a simplified example of an add-on that adds a custom tool to Blender's toolbar. This tool creates a new object in the scene when clicked. Here's a basic outline of the code:

```
bl_info = {

"name": "Custom Tool",

"blender": (2, 80, 0),

"category": "Object",

}

import bpy

class OBJECT_OT_custom_tool(bpy.types.Operator):

bl_idname = "object.custom_tool"

bl_label = "Custom Tool"

bl_options = {"REGISTER", "UNDO"}

def execute(self, context):

bpy.ops.mesh.primitive_cube_add()

return {"FINISHED"}

def menu_func(self, context):

self.layout.operator(OBJECT_OT_custom_tool.bl_idname)

def register():

bpy.utils.register_class(OBJECT_OT_custom_tool)
```

```
bpy.types.VIEW3D_MT_mesh_add.append(menu_func)

def unregister():

bpy.utils.unregister_class(OBJECT_OT_custom_tool)

bpy.types.VIEW3D_MT_mesh_add.remove(menu_func)

if __name__ == "__main__":

register()
```

This add-on creates a custom tool labeled "Custom Tool" in Blender's toolbar. When clicked, it adds a cube object to the scene. Note that this is a simplified example, and real-world add-ons can be much more complex and feature-rich.

8.3.5: Distributing Your Add-on

Once you've developed your add-on, you can distribute it to other Blender users. There are various ways to share your add-on:

- **Blender Market and Gumroad:** You can sell your add-ons on platforms like Blender Market or Gumroad, reaching a wide audience of Blender users.

- **GitHub and GitLab:** Hosting your add-on on version control platforms like GitHub or GitLab allows others to access and collaborate on your code.

- **BlenderArtists.org:** The BlenderArtists community forum has a dedicated section for sharing and discussing add-ons.

- **Blender's Official Add-ons Repository:** If your add-on meets certain criteria and quality standards, you may submit it to Blender's official add-ons repository for inclusion in Blender's official releases.

8.3.6: Learning Resources

To dive deeper into add-on development in Blender, consider exploring the following resources:

- **Blender's Official Documentation:** The official documentation includes guides and tutorials on developing add-ons, explaining various aspects of the process.

- **Online Tutorials:** Many online tutorials and courses cover Blender add-on development, providing step-by-step instructions and examples.

- **Blender Stack Exchange and Blender Artists:** These community forums are excellent places to seek help, ask questions, and share your add-ons with the Blender community.

In summary, creating custom add-ons and plugins in Blender allows you to extend its functionality, automate tasks, and streamline your workflow. Understanding the structure of an add-on, developing your code, and providing clear documentation are key steps in add-on development. Sharing your add-on with the Blender community can be rewarding and beneficial, as it allows others to benefit from your contributions.

Section 8.4: Scripting for Custom Effects and Tools

In Blender, scripting opens up a world of possibilities for creating custom effects and tools that cater to your specific creative needs. Whether you're looking to add unique visual effects, streamline your workflow, or enhance your 3D artistry, this section will guide you through the process of scripting custom effects and tools.

8.4.1: Custom Shader Nodes

Shader nodes in Blender are a powerful tool for creating complex materials and visual effects. By scripting custom shader nodes, you can extend Blender's material system to achieve unique visual effects that might not be achievable with the default shader nodes.

For example, you can script a custom shader node to simulate a specific material, like holographic foil or a stylized cartoon shader. This allows you to reuse the effect across multiple projects and share it with others.

8.4.2: Particle Systems and Dynamics

Scripting can be used to create custom particle systems and dynamics simulations in Blender. For instance, you can script the behavior of particles to create specific effects such as swarming behavior, flocking, or custom physics simulations.

You can also script custom forces and fields to control the motion of particles or objects in a scene. This level of control is valuable when you need precise control over the movement and interaction of elements in your 3D scenes.

8.4.3: Custom Operators

Custom operators are scripts that perform specific actions within Blender. They can be used to automate complex tasks, create custom tools, or add functionality not available through Blender's default interface.

For example, you can script a custom operator to automate a series of modeling operations that you frequently perform, such as creating a specific type of architectural detail. Custom operators are accessible through the "F3" search menu in Blender, making them easily discoverable and usable.

8.4.4: Rigging and Animation Scripts

Rigging and animation in Blender can also benefit from custom scripting. You can create scripts to automate rigging processes, set up custom rigs, or add new animation features.

For instance, you can script a tool that generates a complex rig for a character model with a single click, complete with IK (Inverse Kinematics) constraints, controllers, and facial animation setups. This not only saves time but also ensures consistency in your character animation projects.

8.4.5: Scripting for Add-on Development

As discussed in previous sections, creating add-ons is a powerful way to extend Blender's functionality. When scripting custom effects and tools, consider packaging them as add-ons for easier distribution and use by others.

Add-ons can include a combination of custom shader nodes, operators, panels, and other elements that provide a unified experience to users. Packaging your custom effects and tools as add-ons allows other Blender users to easily install and access your creations.

8.4.6: Collaboration and Sharing

Scripting custom effects and tools in Blender can also open up opportunities for collaboration with other artists and developers. You can share your scripts, effects, and tools with the Blender community, whether through forums, online repositories, or collaborative projects.

Collaboration not only allows you to receive feedback and improve your creations but also contributes to the Blender ecosystem by enriching its library of resources and empowering other artists.

8.4.7: Learning Resources

To explore scripting for custom effects and tools in Blender further, consider the following learning resources:

- **Blender's Official Documentation:** The official documentation includes detailed information on scripting custom effects, tools, and add-ons.

- **Online Tutorials and Courses:** Many online tutorials and courses cover scripting for specific effects, tools, and add-on development in Blender.

- **Blender Community Forums:** Participate in discussions on Blender Stack Exchange, Blender Artists, and other forums to seek advice, share your work, and collaborate with fellow Blender users.

In conclusion, scripting in Blender offers limitless creative possibilities for developing custom effects and tools that enhance your 3D artistry and streamline your workflow. By scripting custom shader nodes, particle systems, operators, rigging tools, and more, you can push the boundaries of what's achievable in Blender and contribute to the Blender community. Whether you're a 3D artist looking to achieve unique visual effects or a developer seeking to create custom tools, Blender's scripting capabilities are a valuable asset in your creative toolkit.

Section 8.5: Community Contributions: Sharing and Utilizing Scripts

The Blender community is a thriving ecosystem of artists and developers who share their knowledge, scripts, and add-ons to enhance the Blender experience for everyone. In this section, we'll explore the importance of community contributions, how to share your own scripts, and how to make the most of the scripts created by others.

8.5.1: Why Community Contributions Matter

Community contributions play a vital role in Blender's growth and evolution. They enrich the software by providing new features, tools, and creative possibilities that cater to a wide range of user needs. Here's why community contributions matter:

- **Diverse Expertise:** The Blender community consists of individuals with diverse backgrounds and expertise, including artists, developers, and technical enthusiasts. This diversity leads to a wealth of innovative ideas and solutions.

- **Constant Improvement:** Continuous development and refinement of scripts and add-ons contribute to

Blender's ongoing improvement. The more people contribute, the more Blender evolves.

• **Accessibility:** Community contributions make complex tasks accessible to a broader audience of artists, even those without extensive programming knowledge. Ready-made scripts and add-ons simplify workflows and enhance productivity.

8.5.2: Sharing Your Scripts

If you've developed useful scripts or add-ons in Blender, sharing them with the community is a great way to give back and receive feedback. Here are steps to share your scripts:

1. **Documentation:** Ensure your scripts have clear and well-documented code. Include comments explaining how the scripts work, what they do, and any necessary instructions for users.
2. **Packaging:** If your script is part of a more extensive add-on, package it accordingly. Add a user-friendly interface, icons, and any necessary assets to provide a polished user experience.
3. **Sharing Platforms:** Share your scripts on platforms such as Blender Artists, GitHub, GitLab, or Blender Market. Each platform has its advantages, from community feedback to version control.
4. **Licensing:** Consider choosing an open-source license that defines how others can use, modify, and distribute your scripts. Popular licenses include GNU GPL, MIT, and Apache.
5. **Promotion:** Promote your scripts through forums, social media, and Blender-related websites. Engaging with the

community helps your scripts gain visibility and reach a wider audience.

8.5.3: Utilizing Community Scripts

Utilizing scripts and add-ons created by other community members can significantly enhance your Blender experience. Here's how to make the most of community-contributed scripts:

- **Browse Repositories:** Explore online repositories like GitHub, GitLab, and Blender Market to discover a wide variety of scripts and add-ons. These repositories often have search and categorization features to help you find what you need.

- **Read Documentation:** Always read the documentation provided with a script or add-on. Documentation explains how to install, use, and customize the tool effectively.

- **Test and Experiment:** Experiment with community-contributed scripts in a safe environment. Some scripts may have specific requirements or compatibility issues, so testing is crucial.

- **Contribute Feedback:** If you encounter bugs, have suggestions for improvements, or find issues with a script, provide constructive feedback to the script's author. This helps improve the quality of the script for everyone.

- **Support Authors:** Consider supporting the authors of scripts or add-ons you find particularly valuable. Some creators offer donation options or premium versions with additional features.

8.5.4: Blender Community Forums

The Blender community forums, including Blender Artists and Blender Stack Exchange, are excellent places to engage with fellow Blender users, share your work, and seek assistance with scripts and add-ons. When using these forums for script-related discussions, keep the following tips in mind:

- **Search Before Posting:** Before creating a new post, search the forums to see if your question or issue has already been addressed. This helps prevent duplicate threads.

- **Be Specific:** When asking for help or sharing scripts, provide specific details about your Blender version, the script's version, and any error messages or issues you're encountering.

- **Follow Forum Rules:** Familiarize yourself with the forum's rules and guidelines. Be respectful and considerate in your interactions with others.

8.5.5: Blender Add-on Community

Blender's add-on community is a dynamic ecosystem where artists and developers collaborate to create and share powerful tools and features. Some notable Blender add-ons that have gained popularity in the community include:

- **Node Wrangler:** A tool for streamlining shader node setups in the Shader Editor.

- **Hard Ops and Boxcutter:** A combination of add-ons that enhance modeling and Boolean operations in Blender.

- **Pro Lighting Skies:** An add-on that simplifies lighting setups for realistic outdoor scenes.

These add-ons and many others have become integral parts of many artists' workflows, demonstrating the impact that community contributions can have on Blender's capabilities.

8.5.6: Giving Back to the Community

Contributing to the Blender community doesn't have to be limited to sharing scripts. You can also give back by answering questions on forums, creating tutorials, participating in open-source projects, or collaborating with other artists and developers on exciting projects.

By actively engaging with the Blender community, you not only benefit from the knowledge and creativity of others but also play a part in shaping the future of Blender and its vast ecosystem of scripts, add-ons, and tools.

In conclusion, the Blender community thrives on the contributions of its members. Whether you're sharing your own scripts or utilizing those created by others, your involvement enhances the Blender experience for everyone. By fostering a collaborative spirit and making the most of community resources, you can take your Blender skills to new heights and contribute to the growth and evolution of this dynamic 3D software.

Chapter 9: Advanced Projects and Techniques

9.1: Crafting Complex Scenes and Environments

In the world of 3D graphics and animation, creating complex scenes and environments is a hallmark of advanced 3D artistry. In this section, we'll delve into the techniques, strategies, and considerations for crafting intricate and visually stunning 3D scenes in Blender.

9.1.1: Conceptualizing Your Scene

Before diving into the technical aspects of scene creation, it's essential to start with a clear concept. What story or message do you want your scene to convey? What is the mood or atmosphere you aim to create? Sketching out your ideas, creating mood boards, or writing down a narrative can help you define the direction of your project.

9.1.2: Scene Layout and Composition

Effective scene layout and composition are critical for guiding the viewer's eye and creating visual interest. Consider the placement of objects, the rule of thirds, leading lines, and focal points to compose your scene. Blender's camera tools and viewport settings can aid in achieving the desired composition.

9.1.3: Modeling and Asset Management

Complex scenes often require numerous 3D models and assets. Organize your modeling process by breaking down objects into manageable pieces. Utilize Blender's grouping, collections, and linking features to keep your scene organized and facilitate easy changes and updates.

9.1.4: Texture and Material Design

Texture and material design bring realism and depth to your scene. Learn how to create custom textures, use image textures, and apply shaders effectively. Experiment with Blender's procedural textures to add details and variation to materials.

9.1.5: Lighting Techniques

Lighting is a key element in scene creation, influencing the mood, tone, and visual appeal. Blender offers various types of lights, including point, spot, area, and sunlight. Explore different lighting setups and techniques, such as three-point lighting and HDRI (High Dynamic Range Imaging) lighting, to achieve your desired results.

9.1.6: Environmental Effects

To make your scene more immersive, consider adding environmental effects like fog, mist, or volumetrics. Blender's volumetric rendering capabilities enable you to simulate atmospheric effects realistically. Experiment with volume shaders and particle systems to achieve the desired environmental atmosphere.

9.1.7: Animation and Interactivity

For scenes that tell a story or require interactivity, animation plays a crucial role. Plan and create animations for objects, cameras, and characters within your scene. Utilize Blender's timeline, keyframing, and graph editor to control motion and timing.

9.1.8: Render Settings and Optimization

Rendering complex scenes can be computationally intensive. Optimize your render settings to strike a balance between quality and render time. Blender provides options for controlling sampling, denoising, and output resolution. You can also explore render farms or cloud rendering services for faster results.

9.1.9: Post-Processing and Compositing

Enhance your scene's final look through post-processing and compositing. Blender's compositor allows you to apply color correction, filters, and effects to your renders. Experiment with node-based compositing to achieve a unique and polished result.

9.1.10: Case Studies

To gain inspiration and insights into crafting complex scenes, study notable projects created by experienced Blender artists. Analyze their techniques, workflows, and decision-making processes. Case studies provide valuable learning opportunities and can spark your creativity.

9.1.11: Collaboration and Feedback

Collaboration with other artists or seeking feedback from peers can elevate your scene creation skills. Sharing your work and receiving constructive criticism can help you identify areas for improvement and refine your project.

9.1.12: Patience and Iteration

Crafting complex scenes often requires patience and iteration. Don't be discouraged by challenges or setbacks. Continuously refine your work, experiment with different approaches, and embrace the learning process.

In summary, crafting complex scenes and environments in Blender is a rewarding journey that combines artistic vision with technical expertise. Whether you aim to create realistic architectural renderings, imaginative fantasy worlds, or captivating animated sequences, the techniques and considerations discussed in this section provide a solid foundation for your advanced 3D projects. Embrace creativity, practice, and persistence as you embark on your journey of scene creation in Blender.

9.2: Advanced Character Design and Development

Advanced character design and development in Blender represent a creative and technical challenge that many 3D artists aspire to conquer. In this section, we will explore the intricacies of creating compelling 3D characters, from initial concept to detailed modeling, texturing, rigging, and animation.

9.2.1: Conceptualizing Your Character

The foundation of any character design begins with a clear concept. Define your character's backstory, personality, and purpose within your project. Create sketches, mood boards, or written descriptions to visualize your character's appearance and traits.

9.2.2: Character Modeling

Character modeling involves translating your concept into a 3D mesh. Start with basic shapes and gradually refine the model's proportions, anatomy, and details. Blender's modeling tools, such as sculpting, extruding, and edge loops, are essential for creating a character's form.

Consider topology, the arrangement of vertices, edges, and faces, to ensure that your character deforms correctly during animation. Proper topology is crucial for achieving realistic and expressive character movement.

9.2.3: Sculpting and Detailing

Sculpting adds fine details and organic forms to your character. Blender's sculpt mode allows you to use brushes to manipulate the geometry and add intricate features like wrinkles, scars, or muscle definition. Sculpting gives your character a more lifelike and visually appealing appearance.

9.2.4: UV Unwrapping and Texturing

UV unwrapping is the process of flattening the 3D model's surface to create a 2D texture map. This map serves as a canvas for applying textures and materials to your character. Planar, cylindrical, and spherical unwrapping methods are commonly used in character texturing.

Textures add color, surface detail, and realism to your character. Use image textures and procedural textures to create skin, clothing, and accessories. Pay attention to specularity, roughness, and normal maps to enhance material realism.

9.2.5: Rigging and Weight Painting

Rigging is the process of creating a skeleton or armature that controls your character's movement. Attach bones to the character's mesh and define how they influence specific vertices through weight painting. Weight painting determines how each bone affects deformation during animation.

Blender offers tools for automatic rigging and skinning, such as the Rigify add-on, which can simplify the rigging process. However, custom rigs offer more control and are often necessary for complex characters.

9.2.6: Facial Rigging and Expressions

Facial rigging is crucial for animating character expressions and emotions. Create a system of bones and controls that allow you to manipulate the character's facial features, including eyes, eyebrows, mouth, and cheeks. Shape keys and drivers can help automate facial expressions.

9.2.7: Animation and Pose Libraries

Animating your character brings it to life. Plan and execute animations that convey your character's personality and story. Blender's animation tools, including keyframing, the graph editor, and the Dope Sheet, provide the necessary control for character animation.

Pose libraries allow you to save and reuse specific poses, making animation more efficient. Character libraries can store various expressions, gestures, and stances that you can easily apply to your character.

9.2.8: Cloth Simulation and Dynamics

For characters wearing clothing or accessories, cloth simulation and dynamics add realism to the animation. Simulate fabric behavior, such as draping, folding, and wrinkling, using Blender's cloth simulation tools. Set up collision objects to interact with the character's clothing.

9.2.9: Rendering and Lighting

Render your character in a visually appealing environment. Experiment with different lighting setups, such as three-point lighting, to highlight your character's features. Pay attention to shadows, reflections, and ambient occlusion to enhance the character's presence in the scene.

9.2.10: Post-Processing and Rendering Effects

After rendering, apply post-processing effects to enhance the final result. Blender's compositor provides tools for color correction, depth of field, bloom, and more. Experiment with these effects to achieve your desired visual style.

9.2.11: Collaboration and Feedback

Collaboration with other artists or seeking feedback from peers can help you refine your character design and animation. Share your work on Blender forums or social media platforms to receive valuable critiques and suggestions for improvement.

9.2.12: Case Studies

To gain inspiration and insights into advanced character design and development, study case studies of exceptional character projects created by experienced Blender artists. Analyze their techniques, rigging setups, animation workflows, and character design principles.

In conclusion, advanced character design and development in Blender require a combination of artistic creativity and technical proficiency. Whether you're creating realistic human characters, fantastical creatures, or animated mascots, the techniques and considerations discussed in this section provide

9.3: Creating Short Films and Animations in Blender

Creating short films and animations in Blender is a captivating and challenging endeavor that allows you to tell stories, convey messages, and showcase your artistic and technical skills. In this section, we will explore the various aspects of producing short films and animations using Blender, from storytelling and pre-production to animation, rendering, and post-production.

9.3.1: Storytelling and Concept Development

Every animation begins with a story or concept. Whether it's a simple character animation or a complex short film, a compelling narrative or idea serves as the foundation. Develop your story, define characters, and establish the message or emotion you want to convey through your animation.

Storyboarding is a valuable tool for visualizing your animation's sequences and camera shots. Create rough sketches or digital storyboards to plan the composition of each scene.

9.3.2: Pre-Production and Planning

Pre-production involves detailed planning before you start creating assets or animating. This phase includes scriptwriting, character design, scene layout, and asset planning. Create a production schedule and budget to ensure a smooth workflow.

9.3.3: 3D Modeling and Asset Creation

Once you have a plan, start creating the 3D models, characters, props, and environments required for your animation. Blender provides versatile modeling tools, sculpting capabilities, and texturing options to bring your assets to life. Pay attention to detail, as well-modeled and textured assets contribute to the overall quality of your animation.

9.3.4: Rigging and Character Animation

Rigging is essential for character animation. Rig your characters with bones and controls to make them poseable. Use inverse kinematics (IK), forward kinematics (FK), and shape keys to animate facial expressions and body movements.

Blender's animation tools, including the timeline, graph editor, and dope sheet, allow you to create keyframe animations, refine timing, and fine-tune movements. Add anticipation, follow-through, and squash-and-stretch to make your animations more dynamic and engaging.

9.3.5: Camera Animation

Animating the camera is crucial for creating cinematic shots and storytelling. Plan camera movements, angles, and transitions that complement your story. Blender's camera settings, tracking, and constraints enable you to achieve smooth and dynamic camera animations.

9.3.6: Lighting and Rendering

Effective lighting enhances the mood and atmosphere of your animation. Experiment with different lighting setups and techniques to achieve the desired look. Blender offers multiple rendering engines, such as Cycles and Eevee, each with its strengths and capabilities. Choose the one that suits your project's requirements.

9.3.7: Sound Design and Music

Sound design, including dialogues, sound effects, and music, adds depth and immersion to your animation. Record dialogues, Foley sound effects, or use royalty-free sound libraries. Compose or license music that complements the mood and enhances the storytelling.

Blender's video sequence editor (VSE) allows you to synchronize sound with your animation, create soundtracks, and add effects.

9.3.8: Post-Production and Editing

Post-production involves editing, compositing, and refining your animation. Use Blender's compositor to apply color correction, add visual effects, and fine-tune the overall look of your animation. Edit sequences, add transitions, and ensure that the pacing aligns with your storytelling.

9.3.9: Export and Distribution

Prepare your animation for distribution by exporting it in the desired format and resolution. Blender supports various video formats, including MP4, AVI, and MOV. Consider rendering multiple versions for different platforms, such as YouTube, Vimeo, or film festivals.

9.3.10: Collaboration and Feedback

Collaborate with other artists and seek feedback from peers during the production process. Collaborative projects can benefit from a shared workload and diverse perspectives. Receiving constructive criticism helps you identify areas for improvement and refine your animation.

9.3.11: Case Studies and Resources

To further your understanding of creating short films and animations in Blender, study case studies of successful Blender animations and films. Analyze their storytelling techniques, animation styles, and production workflows.

Additionally, explore online resources, tutorials, and forums dedicated to Blender animation and filmmaking. Learning from experienced animators and filmmakers can provide valuable insights and techniques to enhance your skills.

In conclusion, creating short films and animations in Blender is a multi-faceted journey that combines storytelling, artistic creativity, and technical expertise. Whether you aspire to create character animations, motion graphics, or narrative short films, Blender offers a versatile and powerful platform to bring your ideas to life. Embrace the creative process, practice, and experimentation as you embark on your animation projects.

9.4: Integrating Blender with Other Software Tools

Integrating Blender with other software tools is a valuable skill that expands your capabilities and enhances your workflow. In this section, we will explore how Blender can be seamlessly integrated with various software applications and pipelines to achieve specific goals and overcome limitations.

9.4.1: Import and Export Formats

Blender supports a wide range of file formats for importing and exporting 3D assets. When working with other 3D software, it's crucial to understand the compatible formats and the potential data loss or conversion issues. Some common formats include FBX, OBJ, Collada (DAE), and Alembic (ABC).

9.4.2: Blender as a Modeler for Other Software

Blender's powerful modeling and sculpting tools make it an excellent choice for creating 3D assets, even if you intend to use them in other software. You can model, texture, and rig characters, props, or environments in Blender and then export them in a format compatible with your target software.

9.4.3: Blender in Game Development

Blender plays a significant role in game development pipelines. Game engines like Unity and Unreal Engine can import Blender files directly, preserving animations, materials, and textures. Blender's ability to export models with LOD (Level of Detail) settings is especially useful for optimizing game performance.

9.4.4: Blender for 3D Printing

Blender is a valuable tool for 3D printing enthusiasts and professionals. You can design intricate 3D models using Blender's modeling and sculpting features and then export them in STL or other compatible formats for 3D printing. Blender also offers tools for checking and preparing models for 3D printing, ensuring they are watertight and error-free.

9.4.5: Video Editing and Post-Production

While Blender is primarily known for 3D modeling and animation, it also includes a robust video sequence editor (VSE). You can use Blender to edit and post-process video footage, add effects, titles, and even 2D animations. This integration can save time by keeping your entire project within one software environment.

9.4.6: Compositing with Other Software

Blender's compositor is a powerful tool for compositing and adding visual effects to your 3D renders. You can export image sequences or passes from other 3D software and composite them in Blender to enhance the final result. Blender's node-based compositing allows for flexibility and creativity in post-processing.

9.4.7: Using Blender with Adobe Creative Cloud

Blender can be integrated into your Adobe Creative Cloud workflow. You can import Blender 3D models into Adobe After Effects and Photoshop for further compositing and manipulation. This integration can be especially useful when working on motion graphics, product visualizations, or animations that require additional 2D post-processing.

9.4.8: Blender and CAD Software

Blender's capabilities extend to the world of Computer-Aided Design (CAD). While Blender is not a dedicated CAD software, it can be used for creating and visualizing CAD models. You can import CAD files into Blender, apply materials and textures, and render them in a more visually appealing way for presentations and animations.

9.4.9: Using Add-ons and Scripts

Blender's flexibility is further enhanced by the availability of add-ons and custom scripts. These extensions can bridge the gap between Blender and other software by providing specialized import/export functions or custom tools for specific tasks. Explore the Blender community and add-on repositories to find tools that streamline your workflow.

9.4.10: Collaboration and Interoperability

Collaborating with artists using different software can be a seamless process when you understand how to integrate Blender with their tools. Maintaining open communication and sharing compatible file formats and assets ensures a smooth workflow and efficient collaboration.

In conclusion, integrating Blender with other software tools is essential for expanding your creative and technical capabilities. Whether you're working on game development, 3D printing, video editing, or collaborating with artists using different software, understanding how to bridge the gap between Blender and other tools can significantly enhance your workflow and broaden your creative horizons. Explore the possibilities and choose the integration methods that best suit your project's needs.

9.5: Case Studies: Notable Projects Created with Blender

In this section, we will delve into several notable projects and artworks created using Blender, showcasing the diverse range of possibilities and applications of this versatile 3D software. These case studies highlight the creativity and innovation of Blender artists and how they have utilized the tool for various projects.

9.5.1: "Agent 327: Operation Barbershop"

"Agent 327: Operation Barbershop" is a well-known Blender animation project that gained recognition for its high-quality production. Created by Blender Institute, this short film features a spy character embarking on a humorous and action-packed mission. The project demonstrated Blender's capabilities for character animation, rendering, and storytelling.

Key Takeaways:

- Blender can be used for creating professional-quality animated short films.

- Blender's powerful animation tools can bring characters to life with humor and personality.

- Collaborative efforts, as seen in this project, involve a team of talented artists working together.

9.5.2: "Spring"

"Spring" is another successful Blender open movie project by Blender Institute. This project showcased Blender's ability to create visually stunning environments and characters. The film tells the story of a shepherd girl and her dog in a magical world filled with vibrant landscapes.

Key Takeaways:

- Blender's capabilities extend to creating breathtaking environments and detailed character models.
- The project emphasized the importance of storytelling and conveying emotions through 3D animation.

9.5.3: "Tears of Steel"

"Tears of Steel" is a Blender Foundation's open movie project that explored the realm of science fiction and visual effects. This project demonstrated Blender's integration with visual effects software and its ability to create realistic compositing and CGI elements within live-action footage.

Key Takeaways:

- Blender can seamlessly integrate with live-action footage, making it a valuable tool for filmmakers and visual effects artists.
- The project highlighted Blender's compositing capabilities and its role in modern filmmaking.

9.5.4: "Sintel"

"Sintel" is another Blender open movie project that showcased Blender's capabilities in creating a fantasy world and telling an emotional and captivating story. This project emphasized character design, rigging, and animation, along with creating a richly detailed fantasy environment.

Key Takeaways:

- Blender excels in character design, rigging, and storytelling for fantasy-themed animations.

- The project demonstrated Blender's versatility in creating both characters and environments.

9.5.5: "Caminandes: Llama Drama"

The "Caminandes" series of short films is known for its humor and charm. These projects highlighted Blender's ability to create engaging and entertaining character animations. "Llama Drama" specifically featured a comical adventure of a llama in a South American setting.

Key Takeaways:

- Blender can be used to create lighthearted and humorous character animations.

- The projects emphasized the importance of character personality and humor in storytelling.

9.5.6: "Cosmos Laundromat"

"Cosmos Laundromat" is a unique Blender open movie project that explored abstract and surreal storytelling. It demonstrated Blender's flexibility in handling unconventional narratives and artistic expressions.

Key Takeaways:

- Blender can be used for experimental and artistic storytelling.

- The project showcased Blender's ability to create abstract and visually striking animations.

These case studies illustrate the wide range of projects and artistic styles that can be achieved using Blender. Whether it's creating realistic characters and environments, integrating Blender with live-action footage, or pushing the boundaries of artistic expression, Blender continues to prove its versatility and relevance in the world of 3D graphics and animation. As you explore your own projects in Blender, draw inspiration from these examples to unleash your creativity and make the most of Blender's capabilities.

10: Preparing for a Career in 3D Graphics

In this chapter, we will explore the steps and considerations for preparing for a career in the field of 3D graphics using Blender as a foundational tool. Whether you aspire to work as a 3D artist, animator, game developer, or in a related role, this chapter provides valuable insights into building your portfolio, networking, and staying updated with industry trends.

10.1: Building a Portfolio with Blender Projects

A strong portfolio is essential for showcasing your skills and attracting potential employers or clients in the 3D graphics industry. Blender can be your primary tool for creating an impressive portfolio. Here are key steps to build a compelling portfolio with Blender projects:

1. **Diverse Project Selection:** Include a variety of projects that demonstrate your versatility. Create 3D models, character animations, architectural visualizations, motion graphics, and other types of content to showcase your

range of skills.

2. **Quality Over Quantity:** Focus on quality rather than quantity. A few exceptional projects are more impactful than many mediocre ones. Spend time refining and perfecting your work.
3. **Storytelling and Emotion:** Consider the narrative and emotional impact of your projects. A well-told story or an emotionally resonant character animation can leave a lasting impression on viewers.
4. **Detail and Realism:** Pay attention to details and realism, especially if you aim to work in fields like architectural visualization or character modeling. High-quality textures, lighting, and materials can make your work stand out.
5. **Collaboration:** Collaborate with other artists or join open projects to gain experience and showcase collaborative work in your portfolio. This demonstrates your ability to work in a team.
6. **Variety of Styles:** Explore different artistic styles to highlight your adaptability. Showcase both realistic and stylized projects to demonstrate your flexibility as an artist.
7. **Problem Solving:** Document challenging projects where you had to solve complex problems. Explain your thought process and the solutions you implemented.
8. **Progression:** Show your growth and development as an artist by including older and newer work in your portfolio. Highlight how you have improved over time.
9. **Personal Projects:** Include personal projects that reflect your unique interests and passion. These can reveal your creativity and dedication.
10. **Presentation:** Pay attention to how you present your portfolio. Use a well-organized website or an online portfolio platform to display your work professionally.

11. **Feedback and Iteration:** Seek feedback from peers and mentors to refine your portfolio. Iterate and improve based on constructive criticism.
12. **Context and Process:** Provide context for your projects. Explain your creative process, the tools and techniques you used, and the challenges you faced. This insight can engage viewers and potential employers.
13. **Contact Information:** Ensure your portfolio includes clear contact information. Make it easy for interested parties to get in touch with you.

By following these steps and continually updating your portfolio with new and impressive Blender projects, you can effectively showcase your talents and increase your chances of success in the 3D graphics industry. Your portfolio is your calling card, so invest time and effort into making it a compelling representation of your skills and creativity.

10.2: Networking and Community Involvement

Networking and active community involvement are crucial aspects of preparing for a successful career in 3D graphics using Blender. Building connections, collaborating with peers, and engaging with the Blender community can open up numerous opportunities and provide valuable support. Here's how you can effectively network and get involved in the Blender community:

1. **Participate in Online Forums and Communities:** Join Blender-related forums, social media groups, and communities where artists and enthusiasts share their work, insights, and experiences. Websites like Blender Artists, Blender Stack Exchange, and BlenderArtists.org

are great places to start. Engage in discussions, ask questions, and share your knowledge.

2. **Attend Blender Conferences and Meetups:** Whenever possible, attend Blender conferences, events, and local meetups. These gatherings offer the chance to meet fellow Blender users, professionals, and even Blender developers. You can gain insights into the latest industry trends and Blender updates while establishing meaningful connections.
3. **Contribute to Open Source Projects:** Blender is an open-source software, and contributing to its development or related projects can enhance your visibility within the community. Whether it's submitting bug reports, creating add-ons, or providing feedback, your contributions are valuable.
4. **Share Your Work Online:** Regularly showcase your Blender projects on platforms like ArtStation, Behance, or your personal website. Share your process, challenges, and successes to attract a wider audience and receive feedback from peers and potential employers.
5. **Collaborate on Projects:** Collaborative projects within the Blender community can be rewarding and help you network. Join or initiate collaborative projects where artists work together to create animations, short films, or games. This not only improves your skills but also introduces you to fellow artists.
6. **Engage with Blender Artists:** Actively engage with fellow Blender artists by offering feedback on their work and seeking their opinions on your projects. Constructive criticism and mutual support can lead to personal and professional growth.
7. **Follow Blender News and Updates:** Stay informed about

Blender's latest developments, updates, and releases. Blender's website and social media channels provide essential information. Being up-to-date allows you to adapt to changes and incorporate new features into your workflow.

8. **Attend Workshops and Webinars:** Many Blender artists and institutions offer workshops and webinars to share knowledge and techniques. Participating in these educational opportunities can enhance your skills and help you connect with instructors and other attendees.
9. **Collaborate on Open Projects:** Blender Foundation periodically runs open movie and open game projects, inviting community members to contribute. Participating in these projects is a great way to work on real-world productions and gain exposure.
10. **Showcase Your Expertise:** If you have specialized skills within the Blender ecosystem, such as scripting or rigging, showcase your expertise through tutorials, documentation, or workshops. Sharing your knowledge can establish you as an authority in your area of expertise.
11. **Participate in Challenges and Contests:** Blender challenges and contests are a fun way to test your skills, learn new techniques, and gain recognition. Participating in these events can boost your visibility and challenge you to improve.
12. **Professional Organizations:** Consider joining professional organizations related to 3D graphics or animation. These organizations often host conferences and networking events, providing opportunities to connect with industry professionals.

Building a robust network and actively participating in the Blender community can lead to job opportunities, collaborations, and valuable friendships. Remember that networking is a two-way street, and offering support and assistance to others can be just as rewarding as receiving it. Building a positive reputation within the Blender community can significantly contribute to your success in the 3D graphics industry.

10.3: Freelancing vs. Studio Work in the Blender Ecosystem

As you prepare for a career in 3D graphics using Blender, one important decision you'll face is whether to pursue freelancing or studio work. Both paths have their merits and challenges, and the choice depends on your preferences, goals, and circumstances. In this section, we'll explore the differences between freelancing and studio work within the Blender ecosystem.

Freelancing

Pros:

1. **Independence:** Freelancing offers a high level of independence. You have the freedom to choose your projects, clients, and work hours. This autonomy allows you to explore a wide range of creative opportunities.
2. **Diverse Projects:** Freelancers often work on diverse projects spanning industries such as advertising, animation, architecture, and game development. This variety can lead to a rich and rewarding portfolio.
3. **Flexibility:** You can work from anywhere, which is particularly appealing if you prefer a remote or nomadic

lifestyle. Freelancers can adapt their schedules to accommodate personal needs and creative inspiration.

4. **Direct Client Interaction:** Freelancers often communicate directly with clients, which can foster strong client relationships and clear project communication.
5. **Potential for High Earnings:** Depending on your skills and reputation, freelancing can offer the potential for high earnings, especially if you specialize in a niche area with high demand.

Cons:

1. **Inconsistent Income:** Freelancers may experience irregular income patterns. Projects can be feast or famine, requiring careful financial planning.
2. **Self-Employment Challenges:** Freelancers must handle administrative tasks like invoicing, taxes, and marketing themselves. This can be time-consuming and requires business acumen.
3. **Client Uncertainty:** Freelancers might encounter challenging clients, late payments, or project cancellations. Managing client relationships and expectations is essential.
4. **Isolation:** Working independently can lead to isolation. Freelancers may miss the camaraderie and collaboration found in a studio environment.

Studio Work

Pros:

1. **Steady Income:** Studio positions typically offer a stable income, with regular paychecks and benefits like health

insurance and retirement plans.

2. **Collaboration:** Studios provide a collaborative environment where you can learn from colleagues, share ideas, and work on large-scale projects. Teamwork can lead to creative synergy and skill development.
3. **Access to Resources:** Studios often have access to advanced hardware, software licenses, and training opportunities that might be cost-prohibitive for freelancers.
4. **Networking:** Studios offer a built-in network of industry professionals, which can lead to future job opportunities and collaborations.
5. **Structured Workflow:** Studio work often follows a structured pipeline, providing clarity on project roles and responsibilities.

Cons:

1. **Less Independence:** Studio artists may have less creative autonomy and project selection. You may work on assignments dictated by the studio's clients or projects.
2. **Fixed Hours:** Studio jobs typically have fixed working hours, which may not suit those seeking flexible schedules.
3. **Office Location:** Studio work often requires a physical presence at the studio's office, limiting remote work opportunities.
4. **Competition:** Securing a studio position can be competitive, with limited job openings and a high demand for experienced artists.

Ultimately, the choice between freelancing and studio work depends on your career goals, lifestyle preferences, financial situation, and risk tolerance. Some artists may opt for freelancing to pursue their passion projects and creative freedom, while others may prefer the stability and resources offered by studios. It's also worth considering hybrid models, such as freelancing while working part-time at a studio, to balance independence and stability. Whichever path you choose, building a strong portfolio and networking within the Blender community will be essential for success in the 3D graphics industry.

10.4: Staying Updated with Industry Trends and Blender Updates

In the dynamic world of 3D graphics and animation, staying updated with industry trends and Blender software updates is crucial for a successful career. Evolving technologies, new techniques, and software improvements can significantly impact your workflow and marketability. Here's how you can effectively stay informed and adapt to changes:

1. Follow Industry News:

Regularly read industry-related publications, websites, and blogs. Websites like BlenderNation, Blender Artists, and industry-specific forums provide valuable updates on trends, tools, and best practices. Subscribe to newsletters and podcasts focused on 3D graphics and animation.

2. Social Media Engagement:

Follow Blender-related accounts and artists on social media platforms like Twitter, Instagram, and YouTube. Artists often share their latest work, tutorials, and insights. Engaging in discussions on social media can also help you connect with peers and industry leaders.

3. Online Courses and Tutorials:

Enroll in online courses, workshops, and tutorials to acquire new skills and techniques. Websites like Udemy, Coursera, and Blender Cloud offer a wide range of courses, from beginner to advanced levels. Learning from industry experts can keep your skills competitive.

4. Conferences and Events:

Attend 3D graphics conferences, conventions, and Blender-related events whenever possible. Events like SIGGRAPH and Blender conferences provide opportunities to learn about the latest developments, network with professionals, and attend presentations and workshops.

5. Blender Foundation's Official Channels:

Stay updated with Blender's official channels, including its website, blog, and social media profiles. The Blender Foundation regularly releases information about software updates, new features, and project developments.

6. User Communities:

Participate in Blender user communities and forums to seek advice, share experiences, and learn from fellow artists. Engaging in discussions can help you discover solutions to challenges and stay informed about industry trends.

7. Experiment and Explore:

Set aside time to experiment with new features and techniques in Blender. Explore the software's capabilities by working on personal projects that challenge your skills and knowledge. Experimentation can lead to creative breakthroughs and skill development.

8. Networking with Peers:

Regularly network with peers, mentors, and professionals in the 3D graphics field. Sharing insights and experiences with others can provide fresh perspectives and keep you aware of emerging trends.

9. Feedback and Critique:

Seek constructive feedback and critique from peers and mentors. Join online forums and art communities where artists provide feedback on each other's work. Constructive criticism helps you grow as an artist and refine your skills.

10. Blender Documentation:

Refer to Blender's official documentation regularly. It provides comprehensive information about Blender's features, tools, and techniques. Staying familiar with the documentation ensures you're aware of all the software's capabilities.

11. Community Projects:

Participate in community-driven Blender projects, such as open movies or game jams. These collaborative efforts not only provide valuable learning experiences but also connect you with other artists and developers.

12. Professional Development:

Invest in continuous professional development. Consider advanced courses, certifications, or workshops to enhance your expertise in specific areas like character rigging, compositing, or VFX.

13. Feedback Loop with Blender Developers:

Stay engaged with Blender's development by providing feedback, reporting bugs, and participating in discussions on Blender's developer forums. Your input can influence the direction of the software and its features.

By actively engaging with these strategies, you can ensure that you remain well-informed and adaptable in the ever-evolving world of 3D graphics and animation. Staying updated not only enhances your skills but also positions you as a knowledgeable and competitive professional within the industry.

10.5: Future Directions and Emerging Technologies in 3D Graphics

The field of 3D graphics is in a constant state of evolution, with emerging technologies and trends shaping its future. As you prepare for a career in 3D graphics using Blender, it's essential to be aware of these developments. Here are some key areas and emerging technologies to keep an eye on:

1. Real-Time Rendering:

Real-time rendering technologies have been advancing rapidly. Game engines like Unreal Engine and Unity are increasingly used for real-time visualization and interactive experiences. Blender's Eevee renderer is also a significant step in this direction, allowing artists to achieve impressive real-time results. The integration of real-time technology into various industries, including architectural visualization and film production, is likely to continue growing.

2. Virtual Reality (VR) and Augmented Reality (AR):

VR and AR technologies are gaining traction in the 3D graphics industry. VR allows for immersive experiences, while AR enhances real-world environments with digital elements. Blender is actively exploring VR support, opening up opportunities for artists to create content for these platforms. As VR and AR become more accessible, demand for skilled artists in this space is expected to rise.

3. AI and Machine Learning:

AI and machine learning are making their mark in 3D graphics. These technologies are used for tasks like procedural content generation, character animation, and realistic simulations. Blender may incorporate AI-driven features in the future, streamlining tasks and enhancing creativity.

4. Realistic Physics and Simulations:

Advancements in physics simulations, particularly in fluid dynamics, smoke, and cloth, are enabling more realistic and dynamic visual effects. Blender's integration of Mantaflow for fluid simulation is an example of this progress. As computational power increases, we can expect even more complex and realistic simulations.

5. GPU Rendering:

GPU rendering has become increasingly popular due to its speed and efficiency. Blender's Cycles and Eevee render engines benefit from GPU acceleration. As GPU technology continues to advance, rendering times will decrease, allowing artists to iterate more quickly.

6. 3D Printing and Fabrication:

3D printing and fabrication technologies are becoming more accessible to artists. Blender's support for 3D printing and its integration with slicer software make it a valuable tool for creating physical objects from digital designs. As 3D printing technologies continue to evolve, artists will have new opportunities in product design and manufacturing.

7. Cross-Platform Collaboration:

Collaboration between artists and developers across different software platforms is becoming easier. Interoperability and open standards are essential for the industry's growth. Blender's commitment to open-source principles aligns with this trend, allowing artists to work seamlessly with other software and collaborate effectively.

8. Environmental and Sustainability Considerations:

The 3D graphics industry is becoming more conscious of environmental and sustainability issues. Artists are exploring ways to reduce the environmental footprint of rendering and production processes. Efficiency improvements and sustainable practices will likely gain prominence.

9. Ethical and Inclusive Design:

There's a growing awareness of the importance of ethical and inclusive design in 3D graphics. Artists are increasingly considering representation, diversity, and cultural sensitivity in their work. This trend reflects a broader societal shift toward inclusivity and responsible content creation.

10. Education and Skill Development:

The demand for skilled 3D artists remains high. Education and skill development in areas like character design, storytelling, and animation will continue to be essential for aspiring artists. Online courses, workshops, and mentorship programs will play a crucial role in nurturing talent.

As you embark on your career in 3D graphics, staying informed about these emerging technologies and trends will help you adapt and thrive in this dynamic field. Embracing new tools and techniques and remaining open to learning and experimentation will be key to your success as a 3D artist using Blender.

Chapter 11: Essential Add-ons and Extensions

11.1 Exploring Popular Blender Add-ons

In this section, we will delve into the world of Blender add-ons and extensions, which enhance and extend the functionality of Blender. Add-ons are like plugins or scripts that can be easily integrated into your Blender workflow. They can streamline your work, introduce new tools, and open up possibilities for various tasks. Let's explore some popular Blender add-ons and how they can benefit your projects.

Blender's Add-on System

Before we dive into specific add-ons, let's first understand how Blender's add-on system works. Blender allows users to install, enable, and disable add-ons easily through the preferences menu. You can also develop your own custom add-ons using Python scripting, which provides incredible flexibility in extending Blender's capabilities.

1. Node Wrangler

Node Wrangler is a must-have add-on for anyone working with the Shader Editor or Compositor in Blender. It simplifies the node-based workflow by providing quick shortcuts and tools to manipulate nodes efficiently. For example, you can easily connect and disconnect nodes, viewer nodes, and perform various operations with just a keystroke.

```
# Example of using Node Wrangler in Python script

import bpy

# Enable Node Wrangler add-on

bpy.ops.preferences.addon_enable(module='node_wrangler')
```

2. Hard Ops

Hard Ops is a powerful modeling and workflow enhancement tool. It offers a wide range of tools for boolean operations, bevels, and mesh management. This add-on is particularly useful for creating complex and detailed models with precision.

```
# Example of using Hard Ops add-on in Python script
```

```
import bpy

# Enable Hard Ops add-on

bpy.ops.preferences.addon_enable(module='hardops')
```

3. Graswald

Graswald is a specialized add-on for creating realistic vegetation and landscapes. It provides a library of high-quality grass, trees, and plants, making it easier to populate your scenes with natural elements. This is a valuable asset for architectural visualization, environmental design, and outdoor scenes.

```
# Example of using Graswald add-on in Python script

import bpy

# Enable Graswald add-on

bpy.ops.preferences.addon_enable(module='graswald')
```

4. BlenderKIT

BlenderKIT is a comprehensive add-on that offers a vast library of 3D assets, materials, and HDRI environments. It simplifies the process of finding and importing assets directly into your Blender projects, saving you time and effort in asset creation.

```
# Example of using BlenderKIT add-on in Python script

import bpy

# Enable BlenderKIT add-on

bpy.ops.preferences.addon_enable(module='blenderkit')
```

5. Rigify

Rigify is an essential add-on for character animators. It provides a powerful rigging system that allows you to easily rig and animate characters with various controls and features. Rigify's modular design makes it adaptable to different character designs and animation needs.

```
# Example of using Rigify add-on in Python script
import bpy
# Enable Rigify add-on
bpy.ops.preferences.addon_enable(module='rigify')
```

These are just a few examples of popular Blender add-ons that can significantly enhance your workflow and project capabilities. The Blender community constantly develops new add-ons, so it's worth exploring the vast add-on ecosystem to find tools that suit your specific needs.

In the next sections, we'll continue to explore different categories of add-ons, customization options, and best practices for using them effectively.

11.2 Customizing Blender with Extensions

In this section, we'll explore the process of customizing Blender through extensions and add-ons. While Blender comes with a wide range of features and tools out of the box, customization allows you to tailor the software to your specific needs and workflow. Whether you're a 3D artist, animator, or game developer, understanding how to customize Blender is essential for optimizing your efficiency and creative output.

The Power of Customization

Blender's open-source nature and Python scripting capabilities make it highly customizable. You can create your own add-ons or install existing ones to extend Blender's functionality. Customization can range from small interface tweaks to creating complex tools for your unique projects.

Creating Custom Shortcuts

One of the most straightforward ways to customize Blender is by creating custom keyboard shortcuts. These shortcuts can significantly speed up your workflow by allowing quick access to frequently used tools and functions. Here's how you can create a custom shortcut in Blender:

1. Go to Edit > Preferences > Keymap.
2. In the Keymap section, you'll see a list of categories and functions that can be assigned shortcuts.
3. Select the category or function you want to create a shortcut for.
4. Click the Add New button.
5. Enter your desired keyboard shortcut combination in the "Key-Binding" field. For example, you can use "Ctrl + Shift + A."
6. In the "Operator" field, you can specify the Blender operation or command you want to assign to this shortcut. For instance, you could assign "Object Mode" or "Subdivide" to this shortcut.
7. You can also choose additional options such as setting the shortcut to be active in specific modes or contexts.
8. Finally, click the Add button to save your custom shortcut.

Customizing the User Interface

Blender allows you to customize its user interface to match your preferences and workflow. You can rearrange panels, adjust the color scheme, and even create custom layouts tailored to different tasks.

1. To customize the user interface, go to Edit > Preferences > Themes.
2. Here, you can choose from existing themes or create your own by modifying the color settings for various interface elements.
3. To rearrange panels and create custom layouts, you can drag and drop panels to different locations within the Blender window. This flexibility allows you to create a workspace that suits your specific needs.

Developing Custom Add-ons

For more advanced customization and automation, you can develop your own custom add-ons using Python scripting. Blender's Python API provides access to nearly every aspect of the software, allowing you to create tools, automate tasks, and extend functionality.

Here's a basic example of a custom add-on that creates a new menu in Blender:

```
import bpy

class SimpleCustomMenu(bpy.types.Menu):

bl_idname = "OBJECT_MT_simple_custom_menu"

bl_label = "Custom Menu"

def draw(self, context):
```

```
layout = self.layout
layout.operator("object.shade_smooth")
layout.operator("object.shade_flat")
def menu_func(self, context):
self.layout.menu("OBJECT_MT_simple_custom_menu")
def register():
bpy.utils.register_class(SimpleCustomMenu)
bpy.types.VIEW3D_MT_object.append(menu_func)
def unregister():
bpy.utils.unregister_class(SimpleCustomMenu)
bpy.types.VIEW3D_MT_object.remove(menu_func)
if __name__ == "__main__":
register()
```

This simple add-on creates a custom menu in Blender's 3D Viewport, offering options to shade objects smoothly or flat. While this is a basic example, it demonstrates how you can extend Blender's functionality to suit your specific needs.

Exploring Existing Add-ons

Beyond creating your own add-ons, you can explore the vast library of existing add-ons developed by the Blender community. Many add-ons are freely available and can be installed directly from Blender's preferences. These add-ons cover a wide range of functionalities, from modeling and animation tools to specialized solutions for architectural visualization and game development.

In summary, customizing Blender through extensions and add-ons empowers you to create a personalized workflow, streamline your tasks, and enhance your creative capabilities. Whether you're a beginner or an experienced Blender user, exploring customization options can significantly improve your efficiency and overall experience with the software.

11.3 Add-ons for Improved Workflow and Efficiency

In this section, we will explore Blender add-ons that are specifically designed to improve your workflow and increase efficiency when working on various tasks within the software. These add-ons offer time-saving features, automation, and enhancements that can significantly benefit both beginners and experienced Blender users.

1. Auto Tile Size

Managing tile sizes for rendering in Blender can be a bit complex, especially when trying to find the optimal balance between speed and quality. The Auto Tile Size add-on automatically calculates and sets the optimal tile size for rendering based on your hardware, which can save you time and ensure optimal results.

```
# Example of using Auto Tile Size add-on in Python script

import bpy

# Enable Auto Tile Size add-on

bpy.ops.preferences.addon_enable(module='auto_tile_size')
```

2. *Asset Flinger*

Asset Flinger is a handy add-on for quickly importing and managing assets in Blender. It provides a library-like interface, allowing you to browse and insert objects, materials, and assets into your scene with ease. This is especially useful when working on complex scenes with many elements.

```
# Example of using Asset Flinger add-on in Python script

import bpy

# Enable Asset Flinger add-on

bpy.ops.preferences.addon_enable(module='asset_flinger')
```

3. *Speedflow*

Speedflow is a comprehensive modeling add-on that significantly accelerates the modeling process in Blender. It offers an array of modeling tools, shortcuts, and features that streamline tasks such as retopology, boolean operations, and more. This add-on is particularly valuable for artists who want to optimize their modeling workflow.

```
# Example of using Speedflow add-on in Python script

import bpy

# Enable Speedflow add-on

bpy.ops.preferences.addon_enable(module='speedflow')
```

4. BoxCutter

BoxCutter is a powerful boolean modeling tool that simplifies the creation of complex shapes and cuts in Blender. It allows you to quickly generate intricate models by performing boolean operations with ease. This is especially useful for hard surface modeling and concept design.

```
# Example of using BoxCutter add-on in Python script

import bpy

# Enable BoxCutter add-on

bpy.ops.preferences.addon_enable(module='box_cutter')
```

5. Mira Tools

Mira Tools is an add-on designed for character rigging and animation. It provides a range of tools and enhancements for rigging, weight painting, and animation, making the character animation process smoother and more efficient.

```
# Example of using Mira Tools add-on in Python script

import bpy

# Enable Mira Tools add-on

bpy.ops.preferences.addon_enable(module='mira_tools')
```

6. RetopoFlow

RetopoFlow is a dedicated retopology add-on for Blender. It offers a suite of tools for creating clean and optimized topology on 3D models. This is particularly useful when working on high-poly models that need to be prepared for animation or rendering.

```
# Example of using RetopoFlow add-on in Python script
import bpy
# Enable RetopoFlow add-on
bpy.ops.preferences.addon_enable(module='retopoflow')
```

7. TextFX

TextFX is an add-on for enhancing text creation and manipulation in Blender. It provides a variety of text effects, animation presets, and styling options that can save you time when working on text-based projects or motion graphics.

```
# Example of using TextFX add-on in Python script
import bpy
# Enable TextFX add-on
bpy.ops.preferences.addon_enable(module='text_fx')
```

These add-ons, among others, can significantly enhance your workflow and efficiency when working in Blender. Whether you're focused on modeling, animation, text, or asset management, exploring and utilizing these tools can make your creative process smoother and more enjoyable. Additionally, many of these add-ons are actively maintained and updated by their developers, ensuring compatibility with the latest Blender versions and features.

11.4 3D Printing and Blender: Add-ons and

Tools

In this section, we'll explore how Blender can be used in the context of 3D printing and discuss relevant add-ons and tools that can aid in the 3D printing workflow. 3D printing is a popular application of Blender, and with the right tools and settings, you can create physical objects from your digital models.

Blender's 3D Printing Toolbox

Blender includes a 3D Printing Toolbox that offers various features and checks to ensure that your 3D models are ready for 3D printing. To access this toolbox, you can follow these steps:

1. Open Blender and switch to the "Layout" workspace.
2. In the "Properties" panel, navigate to the "Output Properties" tab.
3. Scroll down to the "3D Printing" section, where you'll find various tools and options for preparing your model for 3D printing.

3D Printing Add-ons

While Blender's built-in tools are helpful, there are also several add-ons that can enhance your 3D printing workflow. Let's explore a few of them:

1. Mesh Analysis Tools

Mesh Analysis Tools is an add-on that provides advanced analysis and repair tools for 3D printable models. It can help you identify and fix issues like non-manifold geometry, intersecting faces, and other common 3D printing problems.

```
# Example of using Mesh Analysis Tools add-on in Python script

import bpy

# Enable Mesh Analysis Tools add-on

bpy.ops.preferences.addon_enable(module='mesh_analysis_tools')
```

2. Print3D

Print3D is an add-on designed specifically for 3D printing. It offers features like automatic orientation adjustment, support structure generation, and model scaling to ensure a smooth 3D printing process.

```
# Example of using Print3D add-on in Python script

import bpy

# Enable Print3D add-on

bpy.ops.preferences.addon_enable(module='print3d')
```

3. BlenderCAM

BlenderCAM is a powerful add-on for generating toolpaths and G-code for CNC machines, including 3D printers. It allows you to define machining operations and generate paths for milling, cutting, or 3D printing your models.

```
# Example of using BlenderCAM add-on in Python script

import bpy

# Enable BlenderCAM add-on
```

```
bpy.ops.preferences.addon_enable(module='blendercam')
```

Exporting for 3D Printing

To prepare your model for 3D printing, you'll typically need to export it in a format that your 3D printer can understand, such as STL (Stereolithography) or OBJ (Wavefront). Blender supports exporting to these formats and more.

1. Select your model in Blender's 3D Viewport.
2. Go to File > Export > Export as and choose the desired file format.
3. Configure export settings, such as units, scale, and file location.
4. Click the "Export" button to save your 3D printable model.

Checking and Repairing Models

Before sending your model to a 3D printer, it's crucial to check it for potential issues. Blender's 3D Printing Toolbox can help identify problems like non-manifold geometry, holes, and other issues that may lead to printing errors.

To check your model:

1. Ensure that your model is selected in Blender.
2. In the "Properties" panel, navigate to the "Output Properties" tab.
3. Scroll down to the "3D Printing" section and click the "Check All" button.
4. Blender will run a series of checks and provide feedback on any issues found.

If issues are detected, you can use the Mesh Analysis Tools add-on mentioned earlier to help repair them.

By following these steps and utilizing the recommended add-ons, you can leverage Blender's capabilities for 3D printing and ensure that your models are print-ready and error-free. This can save you time and materials while producing high-quality 3D prints.

11.5 Developing Your Own Add-ons: Basics and Best Practices

In this section, we will explore the process of developing your own add-ons for Blender. Creating custom add-ons allows you to extend Blender's functionality to meet your specific needs, automate tasks, and enhance your workflow. Whether you're a Python developer or new to scripting, understanding the basics and best practices for add-on development in Blender is essential.

Getting Started with Python and Blender

Before you dive into creating add-ons, it's crucial to have a basic understanding of Python programming and how it integrates with Blender. Blender provides a Python API that allows you to interact with almost every aspect of the software. Here's how you can get started:

1. **Python Basics**: Familiarize yourself with Python programming by studying its syntax, data types, and common programming concepts. There are numerous online tutorials and resources available for learning Python.
2. **Blender's Python API**: Explore Blender's Python API documentation, which provides details on how to access

and manipulate Blender's data and functionality through Python scripts. You can access this documentation within Blender by going to Help > Python API Reference.

3. **Blender's Text Editor**: Blender includes a built-in text editor for writing and executing Python scripts. You can access it from the "Scripting" workspace in Blender.

Structure of a Blender Add-on

A Blender add-on is essentially a Python script or collection of scripts that extend Blender's functionality. To create an add-on, you need to define its structure and components. Here's a basic outline of what an add-on structure looks like:

```
bl_info = {
"name": "My Custom Add-on",
"blender": (2, 93, 0),
"category": "Object",
}
import bpy
class MyCustomOperator(bpy.types.Operator):
bl_idname = "object.my_custom_operator"
bl_label = "My Custom Operator"
def execute(self, context):
# Your operator logic here
return {'FINISHED'}
```

```
def menu_func(self, context):

self.layout.operator(MyCustomOperator.bl_idname)

def register():

bpy.utils.register_class(MyCustomOperator)

bpy.types.VIEW3D_MT_object.append(menu_func)

def unregister():

bpy.utils.unregister_class(MyCustomOperator)

bpy.types.VIEW3D_MT_object.remove(menu_func)

if __name__ == "__main__":

register()
```

In this example, we define an add-on called “My Custom Add-on” that creates a custom operator for Blender’s “Object” category. The add-on contains a custom operator class (MyCustomOperator) and a registration and unregistration process for the operator and menu integration.

Writing Custom Operators

Operators are the heart of Blender add-ons. They define actions or operations that users can execute within Blender. In the example above, MyCustomOperator is a simple operator that you can customize to perform specific tasks in Blender.

```
class MyCustomOperator(bpy.types.Operator):

bl_idname = "object.my_custom_operator"
```

bl_label = "My Custom Operator"

def execute(self, context):

 # Your operator logic here

return {'FINISHED'}

You can customize the execute method to implement your operator's functionality. This could include creating or modifying objects, changing settings, or performing any other actions within Blender.

Registering and Unregistering

To make your add-on available in Blender, you need to register it when Blender starts and unregister it when Blender exits. The register and unregister functions handle this process:

def register():

bpy.utils.register_class(MyCustomOperator)

bpy.types.VIEW3D_MT_object.append(menu_func)

def unregister():

bpy.utils.unregister_class(MyCustomOperator)

bpy.types.VIEW3D_MT_object.remove(menu_func)

In this example, we use bpy.utils.register_class to register our custom operator class and bpy.types.VIEW3D_MT_object.append(menu_func) to add it to the Object menu.

Best Practices

When developing add-ons for Blender, it's essential to follow best practices to ensure your add-on is stable, maintainable, and user-friendly. Here are some best practices to keep in mind:

- **Naming**: Use clear and descriptive names for your add-on, operators, and classes. This makes it easier for users to understand and use your add-on.

- **Documentation**: Provide clear and concise documentation for your add-on, including how to install, use, and any dependencies it may have.

- **Error Handling**: Implement error handling to gracefully handle unexpected situations and provide informative error messages to users.

- **Testing**: Thoroughly test your add-on in different Blender versions and scenarios to ensure compatibility and reliability.

- **UI Design**: If your add-on includes a user interface, follow Blender's UI design guidelines to create a consistent and user-friendly experience.

- **Versioning**: Keep track of versions and updates to your add-on. Use the bl_info dictionary to specify compatibility with specific Blender versions.

- **Performance**: Optimize your add-on for performance, especially if it involves complex operations or large datasets.

- **Community Engagement**: Engage with the Blender community by sharing your add-on, seeking feedback, and collaborating with other developers.

By following these best practices and continually refining your add-on, you can create a valuable tool for the Blender community and enhance your own productivity as a Blender artist or developer.

Chapter 12: The Blender Ecosystem

12.1 Understanding Blender's Open Source Philosophy

Blender's success and uniqueness in the 3D graphics software world can be attributed in part to its open source philosophy. In this section, we will delve into what this philosophy means for Blender, its community, and the broader 3D graphics industry.

The Essence of Open Source

At its core, open source means that the source code of the software is freely available for anyone to view, modify, and distribute. This approach fosters transparency, collaboration, and community-driven development. Blender adheres to these principles, and its source code can be found on public repositories like GitHub.

Blender's Historical Context

Blender was first developed in the early 1990s by Ton Roosendaal. In 2002, it was open-sourced under the GNU General Public License (GPL), marking a pivotal moment in its history. This decision to open source Blender has had a profound impact on its growth, adoption, and global reach.

Advantages of Open Source for Blender

Blender's open source nature brings several advantages:

1. **Community Collaboration**: Anyone with the skills and knowledge can contribute to Blender's development. This results in a diverse and dedicated community of developers, artists, and enthusiasts who work together to improve the software.
2. **Transparency**: Users can inspect the source code to understand how Blender works at a fundamental level. This transparency builds trust and enables users to identify and fix issues.
3. **Accessibility**: Blender is free to download and use. This lowers the barrier to entry for aspiring 3D artists and students, democratizing access to 3D graphics tools.
4. **Customization**: Open source allows for the creation of custom add-ons and extensions, further enhancing Blender's capabilities and tailoring it to specific workflows.
5. **Stability and Longevity**: Blender's open source model reduces the risk of abandonment or discontinuation. The community ensures its continuous development and improvement.

The Blender Foundation

The Blender Foundation, founded by Ton Roosendaal, plays a central role in Blender's open source ecosystem. It oversees Blender's development, manages funds through donations and merchandise sales, and organizes conferences and events to promote Blender and open source 3D graphics.

The Blender Community

The Blender community is a vibrant and diverse group of artists, developers, educators, and enthusiasts from around the world. This community actively contributes to Blender's growth by providing feedback, creating add-ons, and sharing knowledge through forums, social media, and tutorials.

Blender's Impact on the Industry

Blender's open source philosophy has influenced the broader 3D graphics industry. It has shown that high-quality 3D software can be developed collaboratively and offered for free. This has led to increased competition and innovation in the industry, benefitting both professionals and hobbyists.

Challenges and Opportunities

While Blender's open source model has been a tremendous success, it also faces challenges. Funding development, ensuring sustainability, and managing a growing community are ongoing concerns. However, these challenges also present opportunities for growth and improvement.

In summary, Blender's open source philosophy is a fundamental pillar of its identity. It empowers users, fosters collaboration, and has a lasting impact on the 3D graphics industry. Understanding this philosophy provides valuable context for Blender users and enthusiasts, highlighting the software's unique position in the world of 3D graphics.

12.2 The Blender Foundation and Its Role in

Development

In this section, we will explore the Blender Foundation and its pivotal role in the development, promotion, and support of Blender as an open source 3D graphics software. Understanding the Blender Foundation's mission and activities provides insight into the sustainability and growth of Blender as a powerful tool for artists and developers.

Birth of the Blender Foundation

The Blender Foundation was established in 2002 by Ton Roosendaal, the creator of Blender, and other dedicated individuals. Its primary goal was to support and promote Blender as an open source software project. This marked a significant turning point in Blender's history, as it transitioned from being a closed-source project to an open and community-driven initiative.

Mission and Objectives

The Blender Foundation's mission is to:

1. **Support Blender Development**: The foundation provides funding and resources to support the development of Blender. This includes hiring developers, organizing development sprints, and managing project coordination.
2. **Ensure Blender's Freedom**: The foundation safeguards Blender's open source nature, ensuring that it remains freely available and modifiable by anyone.
3. **Promote Blender's Use**: It actively promotes Blender's use in various industries, from animation and VFX to game development and architectural visualization.
4. **Educational Initiatives**: The foundation supports

educational projects that aim to teach and train individuals in the use of Blender, making it accessible to students and educators worldwide.

Blender Development Fund

One of the primary mechanisms through which the Blender Foundation supports Blender's development is the Blender Development Fund. This fund collects donations from individuals and organizations interested in supporting Blender's growth. The funds are then used to employ full-time developers and fund critical development projects.

Open Source Development

Blender's open source nature means that its source code is freely available for anyone to view and modify. The Blender Foundation manages this codebase, ensuring that it remains open and accessible to the community. This open development model has enabled contributions from developers worldwide and has accelerated Blender's evolution.

The Institute

The Blender Institute is a division of the Blender Foundation responsible for various activities, including open movie projects, research, and training. Notable projects like "Elephants Dream," "Big Buck Bunny," and "Tears of Steel" were produced by the Blender Institute to showcase Blender's capabilities and push the boundaries of open source animation.

Blender Cloud

Blender Cloud is a platform operated by the Blender Institute that provides a range of services, including training, assets, and collaboration tools. Subscribers can access educational content, production-ready assets, and cloud rendering services, further supporting Blender's user base.

Blender's Global Impact

The Blender Foundation's efforts have had a global impact. Blender is used in studios, schools, and independent projects worldwide. It has played a role in the production of animated films, video games, architectural visualizations, and more. Its presence in the creative and educational industries continues to grow.

Challenges and Future Directions

While the Blender Foundation has achieved significant success, it faces ongoing challenges. Maintaining funding for development, addressing the needs of a growing community, and ensuring Blender's long-term sustainability are among the challenges ahead. However, the foundation's commitment to openness, collaboration, and innovation positions Blender for a promising future.

In summary, the Blender Foundation is a driving force behind Blender's development and global presence. Its dedication to open source values, educational initiatives, and community support has made Blender a powerful and accessible tool for 3D artists and developers worldwide. Understanding the foundation's role provides context for Blender's evolution and continued success in the 3D graphics industry.

12.3 Contributing to Blender's Development

Contributing to Blender's development is not only an opportunity to give back to the community but also a way to shape the future of the software. In this section, we'll explore how individuals and organizations can get involved in the development of Blender, whether through coding, testing, or other forms of support.

The Open Development Model

Blender's development is characterized by its open and collaborative nature. The source code is hosted on platforms like GitHub, making it accessible to anyone interested in contributing. This open development model has led to a diverse and engaged community of developers worldwide.

Ways to Contribute

1. **Coding**: If you have programming skills, you can contribute to Blender by writing code. Blender is primarily developed using Python and C/C++. The Blender Developer Documentation[1] provides guidelines and resources for developers.
2. **Bug Reporting**: Identifying and reporting bugs is a valuable contribution. You can report issues you encounter on Blender's bug tracker[2].
3. **Testing**: Testing Blender's alpha and beta releases is crucial for identifying issues and providing feedback. This helps ensure stable and reliable releases.
4. **Documentation**: Good documentation is essential for

---

1. https://developer.blender.org/

2. https://developer.blender.org/maniphest/task/edit/form/1/

users and developers. You can help improve documentation by contributing to the Blender Manual[3].

5. **User Interface Design**: Blender's user interface is continually evolving. If you have experience in UI/UX design, your insights can contribute to making Blender more user-friendly.
6. **Add-ons**: Developing and sharing add-ons is another way to contribute. You can create add-ons that enhance Blender's functionality and share them with the community.
7. **Financial Support**: Donations to the Blender Development Fund provide critical funding for full-time developers and development projects. Even small donations make a difference.

The Blender Development Fund

The Blender Development Fund is a central mechanism for funding Blender's development. Donations from individuals and organizations go towards employing developers, organizing development sprints, and supporting critical projects. Contributions to the fund directly impact Blender's progress.

Development Sprints

Development sprints are focused periods during which developers work intensively on specific projects or features. These sprints can be organized by the Blender Foundation or by the community. Developers gather to collaborate, code, and address important development goals.

3. https://docs.blender.org/manual/en/latest/

Blender's Licensing

Blender uses the GNU General Public License (GPL), which ensures that it remains open source. This license grants users the freedom to use, modify, and distribute Blender as they see fit, provided they adhere to the GPL's terms.

Code Review and Collaboration

Contributors to Blender submit their changes as patches for review. Experienced developers review and test these patches before they are merged into the main codebase. This rigorous process ensures code quality and stability.

The Blender Community

The Blender community is a diverse and active group of artists, developers, educators, and enthusiasts. Engaging with the community through forums, social media, and events provides opportunities for collaboration and learning.

Challenges and Rewards

Contributing to Blender's development can be challenging, as it requires time and effort. However, the rewards are substantial. You become part of a global community that shares your passion for 3D graphics. Your contributions help shape the future of Blender, making it a more powerful and accessible tool for everyone.

In conclusion, contributing to Blender's development is a meaningful way to support the software and the community. Whether through coding, testing, documentation, or financial support, your contributions play a vital role in Blender's growth and evolution as an open source 3D graphics solution.

12.4 Blender Conferences and Meetups

Blender conferences and meetups serve as vital forums for the Blender community to come together, share knowledge, showcase projects, and collaborate on ideas. In this section, we'll explore the significance of these events and how they contribute to Blender's development and community growth.

Blender Conferences

Blender conferences, often referred to as "BlenderCons," are annual gatherings of Blender enthusiasts, artists, developers, educators, and professionals. These events provide a platform for attendees to:

- **Network**: BlenderCons offer opportunities to meet fellow Blender users, developers, and industry professionals, fostering connections and collaborations.

- **Learn**: Conferences feature presentations, workshops, and tutorials on a wide range of Blender-related topics, including art, animation, development, and more.

- **Showcase Work**: Artists and creators can showcase their Blender projects, animations, and artwork, gaining recognition and feedback from the community.

- **Stay Informed**: Attendees can learn about the latest Blender developments, upcoming features, and industry trends directly from Blender developers and experts.

Blender Conference History

The Blender Conference has a rich history, with its first edition held in 2002. Since then, it has grown significantly in size and importance. The conference typically takes place in Amsterdam, Netherlands, where the Blender Institute is located. It attracts attendees from around the world and has become a focal point for the Blender community.

Blender Conference 2.8

Blender Conference 2.8 was a significant milestone, held in 2019, coinciding with the release of Blender 2.80, a major update with a redesigned interface and numerous new features. The conference celebrated this release and provided in-depth insights into the changes and improvements made.

Blender Conferences Worldwide

While the Amsterdam conference is the most prominent, Blender enthusiasts worldwide organize their own local Blender conferences and meetups. These events cater to specific regions, languages, and interests. They provide a localized platform for users to connect and share their Blender experiences.

Blend4Web Conference

The Blend4Web Conference is a notable event that focuses on the Blend4Web framework for creating interactive 3D web content using Blender. It showcases the capabilities of Blend4Web and its integration with Blender.

Meeting the Developers

One of the unique aspects of Blender conferences is the opportunity to meet the developers behind the software. Developers give presentations, participate in discussions, and engage with the community. This direct interaction between users and developers fosters a sense of collaboration and transparency.

Blender Meetups

In addition to conferences, Blender meetups are smaller, informal gatherings organized by local communities or user groups. Meetups provide a more intimate setting for Blender users to:

- **Share Tips and Tricks**: Attendees can share their Blender tips and tricks, helping each other improve their skills.

- **Discuss Projects**: Artists and developers can discuss ongoing projects, get feedback, and seek advice from peers.

- **Learn from Experts**: Local experts often give talks or workshops, offering valuable insights and knowledge.

- **Inspire Creativity**: Meetups can be a source of inspiration, motivating attendees to explore new creative possibilities with Blender.

Benefits of Blender Conferences and Meetups

Blender conferences and meetups have several benefits:

- **Community Building**: These events strengthen the Blender community by connecting users, artists, developers, and enthusiasts.

- **Knowledge Sharing**: Attendees gain new skills and knowledge through presentations, workshops, and discussions.

- **Project Showcases**: Artists can showcase their work, and developers can present their projects, garnering feedback and recognition.

- **Networking**: Attendees can network with professionals in the industry, potentially opening doors to career opportunities.

- **Feedback Loop**: Direct interaction with developers allows users to provide feedback, request features, and gain insights into Blender's development roadmap.

- **Inspiration**: Being part of a passionate community can inspire attendees to create new and innovative Blender projects.

In conclusion, Blender conferences and meetups are integral to the Blender ecosystem. They provide valuable opportunities for learning, networking, and collaboration, enriching the Blender community and contributing to the software's growth and development. Whether you're a beginner or an experienced Blender user, participating in these events can be a rewarding experience.

12.5 The Future of Blender: Predictions and Trends

The future of Blender is an exciting and ever-evolving landscape. In this section, we'll explore some predictions and emerging trends that may shape the trajectory of Blender as a 3D graphics software and the broader world of 3D artistry.

Continued Growth in Popularity

Blender's user base has been steadily growing, thanks to its open source nature, robust features, and active community. This trend is expected to continue as more artists, students, and professionals discover and adopt Blender as their preferred 3D software. Blender's accessibility and cost-effectiveness make it an attractive choice for newcomers and small studios.

Integration of AI and Machine Learning

The integration of artificial intelligence (AI) and machine learning (ML) technologies into Blender is a promising area of development. These technologies have the potential to enhance various aspects of 3D graphics, from automated character rigging to intelligent scene composition and realistic physics simulations. Blender's open source nature allows for experimentation and innovation in this domain.

Real-Time Rendering and VR

Real-time rendering and virtual reality (VR) experiences are becoming increasingly important in the 3D industry. Blender is poised to keep up with this trend by improving its real-time rendering capabilities and VR support. This will enable artists and designers to create immersive and interactive 3D content more easily within Blender.

Improved Collaboration Tools

As remote work and collaboration across borders become more common, Blender is likely to invest in improving collaboration features. Enhanced version control, asset management, and real-time co-authoring tools could empower artists and teams to work seamlessly on complex projects.

Enhanced Simulation and Physics

Blender's simulation capabilities are expected to see continuous improvement. This includes more advanced physics simulations for fluid, smoke, cloth, and soft bodies. These enhancements will benefit industries like animation, visual effects, and game development, where realistic simulations are crucial.

Increased Industry Adoption

Blender is already gaining traction in professional studios and industries beyond traditional animation and VFX. Its adaptability and open source nature make it a viable option for architectural visualization, product design, medical visualization, and more. As Blender continues to mature and evolve, its adoption in these industries is likely to grow.

Further Integration with Industry Standards

Blender's developers are keen on ensuring compatibility with industry standards. This includes improved import/export support for popular formats like FBX and Alembic, making it easier for Blender to fit seamlessly into existing pipelines and workflows.

Educational Initiatives

Blender's role in education is expected to expand. With more schools, universities, and online courses incorporating Blender into their curricula, the software will play a key role in training the next generation of 3D artists, animators, and developers.

Accessibility and Usability

Usability and user-friendliness are priorities for Blender's development. Efforts to streamline workflows, improve the user interface, and enhance documentation will continue to make Blender more accessible to a wider audience.

Diverse Ecosystem of Add-ons

The Blender add-on ecosystem is set to thrive. As more developers create and share add-ons, Blender users will have access to a diverse range of tools and extensions to customize their workflows and expand Blender's capabilities.

In conclusion, the future of Blender is marked by growth, innovation, and a commitment to open source values. While the specific developments may vary, Blender's journey will continue to be guided by the needs and creativity of its passionate community. As it evolves to meet emerging trends and challenges, Blender remains a powerful and accessible tool for 3D graphics and artistry.

Chapter 13: Architectural Visualization

13.1 Introduction to Architectural Visualization in Blender

Architectural visualization is a prominent application of 3D graphics, and Blender is a powerful tool for creating stunning architectural renders and animations. In this section, we will introduce the concept of architectural visualization and how Blender can be used effectively in this field.

What is Architectural Visualization?

Architectural visualization, often abbreviated as ArchViz, is the process of creating 3D representations of architectural designs. It serves multiple purposes, including:

- **Design Communication**: Architects and designers use visualization to convey their ideas to clients, stakeholders, and construction teams. It helps everyone involved in a project to understand the proposed design.

- **Marketing**: Real estate developers and property sellers use architectural visualization to market properties before they are built. High-quality visualizations can help potential buyers or investors visualize the final product.

- **Analysis**: Visualization can assist in analyzing aspects like lighting, interior layouts, and spatial relationships within a building design.

- **Historical Reconstruction**: In historical preservation and reconstruction, visualization can recreate buildings and structures as they appeared in the past, providing valuable insights for restoration projects.

Blender's Role in Architectural Visualization

Blender's comprehensive toolset makes it an excellent choice for architectural visualization. Here are some key features that make Blender suitable for this purpose:

1. **Modeling Capabilities**: Blender's modeling tools allow users to create detailed and accurate 3D representations of architectural designs. This includes modeling architectural elements such as walls, floors, windows, doors, and furniture.
2. **Realistic Materials**: Blender's material system enables the creation of realistic textures and materials for surfaces, including wood, stone, glass, and metal.
3. **Lighting Control**: Lighting plays a crucial role in architectural visualization. Blender provides control over various types of lights, such as point lights, area lights, and sunlight simulation, to achieve realistic lighting conditions.
4. **Rendering Engines**: Blender supports powerful rendering engines like Cycles and Eevee, which can produce photorealistic images and animations. These engines can simulate materials, lighting, and reflections accurately.
5. **Camera Control**: Blender's camera system allows users to set up precise camera angles and movements for creating compelling visualizations and walkthroughs.
6. **Post-Processing**: Blender's compositing and post-processing capabilities enable users to enhance the final output with effects like depth of field, color grading, and lens flares.

7. **Animation**: Blender can create animated walkthroughs and fly-throughs of architectural designs, making it easier to communicate the spatial aspects of a project.
8. **Interactive Experiences**: With the integration of real-time engines like Unreal Engine or Unity, Blender can be used to create interactive architectural experiences and virtual reality (VR) walkthroughs.

Workflow in Architectural Visualization

A typical workflow in architectural visualization using Blender involves the following steps:

1. **Import or Create 3D Models**: Architects can either import 3D models from architectural software like SketchUp or create them from scratch in Blender.
2. **Texturing and Material Assignment**: Surfaces are assigned appropriate textures and materials to achieve realistic appearances.
3. **Lighting Setup**: Lighting is carefully set up to replicate real-world lighting conditions, considering factors like time of day and weather conditions.
4. **Camera Placement**: Cameras are positioned to capture the best angles and views of the architectural design.
5. **Rendering**: High-quality renders or animations are generated using Blender's rendering engines.
6. **Post-Processing**: The final output may undergo post-processing to enhance its visual quality.
7. **Presentation**: The visualizations are presented to clients, stakeholders, or the public for feedback and approval.
8. **Iterative Refinement**: Feedback and revisions are incorporated into the design, and the process may iterate

until the design is finalized.

Industry Applications

Architectural visualization using Blender is widely applied in various industries:

- **Architecture and Construction**: Architects and construction firms use visualization to present designs to clients and contractors, aiding in project planning and execution.
- **Real Estate**: Real estate developers use visualizations to market properties, especially before construction is completed.
- **Interior Design**: Interior designers can create detailed 3D representations of interior spaces to explore different design options.
- **Heritage Preservation**: Visualization is used in the preservation and reconstruction of historical buildings and cultural heritage sites.
- **Urban Planning**: Urban planners visualize proposed urban developments and infrastructure projects.
- **Entertainment**: Film and game industries use architectural visualization for creating realistic virtual worlds and set designs.

In summary, architectural visualization is a critical field that leverages Blender's capabilities to create immersive 3D representations of architectural designs. Blender's tools for modeling, materials, lighting, and rendering make it a versatile and powerful choice for architects, designers, and visualization professionals in various industries.

13.2 Techniques for Creating Realistic Architectural Models

Creating realistic architectural models is a fundamental aspect of architectural visualization. In this section, we will explore various techniques and best practices in Blender for achieving lifelike architectural models.

Reference Images and Plans

Before you start modeling, it's essential to gather reference images and architectural plans of the building or space you intend to recreate. These references serve as the foundation for your model and help ensure accuracy in proportions and details.

Modeling Workflow

Blender offers a range of modeling tools to create architectural elements effectively. Here's a typical workflow:

1. **Block Out**: Begin by creating simple geometric shapes to represent the building's basic structure. These shapes serve as the initial blocks for your model.
2. **Detail Modeling**: Gradually refine the geometry by adding details such as windows, doors, columns, and other architectural features. Blender's precision modeling tools like snapping and grid snapping can be invaluable here.
3. **Modifiers**: Utilize Blender's modifiers to expedite

modeling tasks. For example, the Array modifier can replicate elements like windows or columns across a facade, saving time and maintaining consistency.

4. **UV Mapping**: When adding textures and materials, ensure that you UV unwrap your model correctly. UV mapping allows textures to be applied accurately to surfaces, enhancing realism.

Realistic Materials and Textures

Materials and textures play a significant role in achieving realism in architectural models:

- **PBR Materials**: Physically Based Rendering (PBR) materials mimic how light interacts with real-world surfaces. Blender supports PBR materials, allowing you to create materials that behave realistically under various lighting conditions.

- **Texture Maps**: Use texture maps, such as diffuse, normal, specular, and roughness maps, to add surface detail and variation to materials.

- **Material Library**: Consider building a library of reusable materials specific to architectural modeling. This can save time on future projects and ensure consistency.

- **Procedural Textures**: Blender's procedural textures enable you to generate complex patterns and surfaces procedurally. These can be particularly useful for creating materials like bricks, tiles, and wood.

Lighting and Environment

Achieving realistic lighting in architectural models is crucial for creating convincing visualizations:

- **HDRi Lighting**: High Dynamic Range images (HDRi) provide realistic and dynamic lighting setups. Blender allows you to use HDRi images as environment lighting sources.

- **Physical Sun and Sky**: Blender's Cycles renderer features a physical sun and sky system, which simulates sunlight accurately based on geographic location and time of day.

- **Artificial Lighting**: For interior scenes, place artificial lights like lamps and ceiling lights realistically. Blender's IES (Illuminating Engineering Society) lighting profiles can replicate real-world lighting patterns.

Camera Setup

Setting up the camera is essential for creating appealing architectural renders:

- **Composition**: Pay attention to composition principles like rule of thirds, leading lines, and framing to create visually engaging shots.

- **Depth of Field**: Use Blender's depth of field settings to control focus and create realistic blur effects for background and foreground elements.

- **Camera Lenses**: Blender allows you to simulate various camera lenses, such as wide-angle or telephoto, to achieve specific visual effects.

Real-Time Rendering

To visualize your architectural models interactively, consider using real-time rendering engines like Eevee or exporting your models to external real-time engines like Unreal Engine or Unity. Real-time rendering provides instant feedback and facilitates immersive experiences for clients and stakeholders.

Quality Control and Testing

Regularly test your architectural models by rendering them from different camera angles and lighting conditions. This helps identify issues with geometry, materials, or lighting that need improvement.

In conclusion, creating realistic architectural models in Blender requires a combination of careful planning, precise modeling, realistic materials, and attention to lighting and camera setup. Blender's versatile toolset empowers architects and visualization professionals to produce lifelike representations of architectural designs, aiding in effective communication and presentation of projects.

13.3 Lighting and Rendering for Architectural Scenes

Lighting and rendering are critical aspects of architectural visualization, greatly influencing the quality and realism of the final result. In this section, we will explore techniques and considerations for achieving effective lighting and rendering in Blender for architectural scenes.

Natural Lighting

For outdoor architectural scenes, natural lighting plays a significant role in creating a realistic atmosphere. Here are some tips for utilizing natural lighting in Blender:

- **Sun Position**: Blender's Cycles renderer includes a physical sun and sky system. You can set the sun's position based on real-world data to simulate accurate lighting conditions for a specific location and time.

- **Sun Angle**: Adjust the angle of the sun to control the direction of shadows and the warmth of sunlight. Blender's sun angle settings allow you to create different times of day, from morning to evening.

- **HDRi Environments**: High Dynamic Range images (HDRi) provide realistic lighting environments for architectural scenes. Use HDRi images that match the desired mood and location of your scene. Blender supports HDRi lighting through its world shader settings.

Artificial Lighting

For indoor and nighttime scenes, artificial lighting becomes crucial. Blender offers various tools for creating realistic artificial lighting setups:

- **Lamp Types**: Blender provides different types of lamps, including point, sun, spot, area, and emission lamps.

Choose the appropriate lamp type based on the scene requirements.

- **IES Profiles**: When simulating real-world artificial lighting fixtures, consider using IES profiles. These profiles contain data about how a specific light fixture distributes light. Blender supports IES profiles, allowing you to recreate accurate lighting patterns.

- **Light Intensity**: Adjust the intensity of artificial lights to match the desired level of illumination. Experiment with brightness and color temperature to achieve the desired ambiance.

Ambient Occlusion and Global Illumination

Ambient occlusion (AO) and global illumination (GI) are rendering techniques that contribute to realism in architectural scenes:

- **Ambient Occlusion**: AO simulates the soft shadows that occur in areas where objects are close to each other. Enabling AO in Blender's render settings can add depth and realism to your scenes.

- **Global Illumination**: GI models the indirect bounce of light in a scene, accounting for how light reflects off surfaces and illuminates nearby objects. Blender's Cycles renderer naturally handles GI, while Eevee offers approximate GI solutions.

Material Setup

Materials play a crucial role in the interaction between light and surfaces. Here are some considerations for materials in architectural scenes:

- **Realistic Textures**: Use high-quality textures that replicate real-world materials. Pay attention to factors like reflectivity, roughness, and color accuracy.

- **Material Consistency**: Ensure consistency in material properties across your scene. Materials should behave similarly in different lighting conditions.

- **Glass and Transparency**: Architectural scenes often include glass elements. Use the principled shader in Blender to create realistic glass materials with appropriate refraction and reflection.

Camera Settings

Camera settings greatly affect the final render:

- **Depth of Field**: Use depth of field to control which parts of the scene are in focus. Adjust the focus distance and f-stop to achieve desired blur effects for background and foreground elements.

- **Exposure**: Control exposure settings to achieve the desired brightness and contrast in your render. Blender allows you to adjust exposure values, ISO, and shutter speed.

Post-Processing

Post-processing can enhance the visual quality of your architectural renders:

- **Color Correction**: Adjust color balance, contrast, and saturation to achieve the desired look in post-processing software like Blender's compositor or external applications like Adobe Photoshop.

- **Bloom and Glare**: Add bloom and glare effects to simulate camera artifacts and enhance the overall appearance of light sources.

- **Lens Effects**: Experiment with lens effects such as vignetting and lens distortion to achieve specific visual styles.

In conclusion, achieving effective lighting and rendering in architectural scenes requires a combination of natural and artificial lighting techniques, attention to materials and camera settings, and post-processing for final adjustments. Blender's versatile tools and rendering engines offer a wide range of possibilities for creating realistic and visually stunning architectural visualizations.

13.4 Creating Virtual Walkthroughs and Tours

Virtual walkthroughs and tours are powerful tools for presenting architectural designs, allowing clients and stakeholders to experience a space as if they were physically there. In this section, we will explore how to create virtual walkthroughs and tours in Blender for architectural visualization.

Benefits of Virtual Walkthroughs

Virtual walkthroughs offer several advantages in architectural visualization:

- **Immersive Experience**: Clients can explore the architectural design in a more immersive way, getting a better sense of scale and spatial relationships.

- **Realistic Visualization**: Virtual walkthroughs provide a realistic representation of lighting, materials, and textures, allowing clients to see how the space will look and feel.

- **Design Feedback**: Stakeholders can provide feedback on design elements, allowing for revisions and improvements before construction begins.

- **Marketing and Pre-Sales**: Virtual tours can be used for marketing purposes, allowing potential buyers or investors to explore properties before they are built.

Blender for Virtual Walkthroughs

Blender offers the tools and capabilities needed to create interactive virtual walkthroughs and tours:

- **Camera Animation**: Blender allows you to animate the camera's position and orientation, creating smooth camera movements through the architectural space.

- **Navigation**: You can provide navigation controls for users to move the camera forward, backward, and turn left or right to explore the environment.

- **Interactivity**: Blender's Game Engine (BGE) or external game engines like Unreal Engine or Unity can be used to add interactive elements such as clickable hotspots, doors that open, or lights that can be turned on and off.

- **Real-Time Rendering**: Real-time rendering engines like Eevee in Blender or external engines offer instant feedback and realistic rendering during the walkthrough.

Workflow for Virtual Walkthroughs

Here's a general workflow for creating virtual walkthroughs in Blender:

1. **Model the Scene**: Create the 3D architectural model of the space you want to showcase, including all relevant details and interior furnishings.
2. **Camera Setup**: Set up the camera that will be used for the walkthrough. Decide on the starting position and angle.
3. **Camera Animation**: Animate the camera's movement through the space. Keyframe the camera's location and orientation at each point along the path.
4. **Navigation Controls**: Implement navigation controls to allow users to move the camera during the walkthrough. This can be done using logic bricks in Blender's Game Engine or scripts in other game engines.
5. **Interactivity**: Add interactive elements if desired. For example, you can set up clickable hotspots that trigger actions, such as opening doors or turning on lights.
6. **Real-Time Rendering**: If you are using real-time engines like Eevee, configure the rendering settings to achieve the desired visual quality during the walkthrough.

7. **Export and Playback**: Export the walkthrough as a video or interactive application, depending on your presentation needs. Blender can export video files, while game engines can create standalone applications.
8. **Testing and Feedback**: Test the virtual walkthrough to ensure it works smoothly and provides a realistic experience. Collect feedback from clients and stakeholders for further refinements.

External Game Engines

While Blender's real-time rendering capabilities are impressive, some users prefer to export their architectural models to external game engines for more advanced interactivity and visual effects. Unreal Engine and Unity are popular choices for this purpose. These engines offer advanced features like physics simulations, advanced lighting, and real-time global illumination.

VR and AR Integration

For an even more immersive experience, consider integrating virtual reality (VR) or augmented reality (AR) technologies into your architectural walkthroughs. Blender can export models and animations that are compatible with VR and AR platforms, allowing users to experience architectural designs in a highly immersive manner.

In conclusion, creating virtual walkthroughs and tours in Blender is a valuable technique for architectural visualization. It allows clients and stakeholders to explore architectural designs in a realistic and interactive way, providing a deeper understanding of the space and fostering collaboration and feedback during the design phase. Whether using Blender's real-time capabilities or exporting to external game engines, virtual walkthroughs can significantly enhance the presentation of architectural projects.

13.5 Case Studies: Notable Architectural Projects in Blender

Examining real-world case studies of architectural projects created with Blender provides valuable insights into the capabilities and versatility of the software for architectural visualization. In this section, we will explore a few notable architectural projects that have leveraged Blender for their visualization.

The "Glass House" by ArchViz Artist

Architectural visualization artist Alex Hogrefe is renowned for his "Glass House" project. This project showcases a modern, minimalist house with an emphasis on transparency and open spaces. Blender was used extensively to create detailed 3D models of the house's architecture, interiors, and surrounding landscape. The project demonstrates Blender's modeling capabilities and its ability to handle complex glass materials and lighting setups.

"The Biodome" by Bronx Zoo

The Wildlife Conservation Society's Bronx Zoo in New York utilized Blender for the visualization of their ambitious "The Biodome" project. This undertaking involved designing a massive indoor rainforest habitat for various animal species. Blender was employed to create 3D models of the biodome's architecture, tropical vegetation, and animal enclosures. The software's ability to handle large-scale environmental designs and realistic materials was crucial in conveying the project's vision.

"L'Arbre Blanc" by Sou Fujimoto Architects

The "L'Arbre Blanc" (The White Tree) residential tower designed by Sou Fujimoto Architects in France is an iconic architectural project. Blender played a significant role in visualizing the tower's unique design, characterized by its tree-like branching balconies and stunning views of the city. Blender's modeling capabilities were instrumental in creating the intricate balconies and the tower's overall form. Additionally, the software allowed for the accurate representation of materials and lighting conditions in the cityscape.

"The Wave" by AS+GG Architects

Adrian Smith + Gordon Gill Architecture's "The Wave" is a conceptual mixed-use development project that envisions a series of wave-shaped buildings along a waterfront. Blender was used to create the 3D models of the buildings, demonstrating its versatility in handling complex architectural shapes. The software's rendering capabilities were leveraged to produce striking visualizations of the project, showcasing how Blender can bring imaginative architectural concepts to life.

"The Hive" by Studio Gang Architects

Studio Gang Architects' "The Hive" project reimagines the concept of a beehive-inspired building. Blender played a pivotal role in modeling the organic shapes and intricate details of the beehive structures. The software's ability to handle unconventional architectural forms and its powerful sculpting tools were key in realizing the project's vision. Blender's rendering capabilities were used to create compelling visuals of the beehive structures in different lighting conditions.

Conclusion

These case studies highlight the diverse range of architectural projects that have successfully utilized Blender for visualization. From modern houses to ambitious wildlife habitats and innovative tower designs, Blender has proven its versatility in handling various architectural styles and scales. Its modeling, material rendering, and visualization capabilities make it a valuable tool for architects, designers, and visualization professionals in bringing architectural visions to life. These examples underscore Blender's significance in the world of architectural visualization and its potential to push the boundaries of architectural design.

Chapter 14: Motion Graphics and Design

14.1 Using Blender for Motion Graphics

Blender is not only a powerful tool for 3D modeling and rendering but also a versatile platform for creating motion graphics and animations. In this section, we will explore how Blender can be used effectively in the field of motion graphics and design.

Motion Graphics and Blender

Motion graphics involve the use of animation, visual effects, and typography to convey a message or tell a story. Blender offers several features that make it suitable for motion graphics:

- **Animation Tools**: Blender's robust animation tools allow for the creation of keyframe animations, including both 2D and 3D animations. The timeline, graph editor, and dope sheet provide precise control over animation timing and curves.

• **Particle Systems**: Blender's particle systems can be used to create dynamic and visually appealing effects like smoke, fire, rain, and more. These systems can be harnessed for motion graphic elements.

• **Physics Simulations**: Blender supports physics simulations for various phenomena, such as fluid dynamics, cloth simulations, and soft body dynamics. These simulations can be integrated into motion graphics to add realism and dynamism.

• **Text and Typography**: Blender offers powerful text editing capabilities, making it suitable for creating animated titles, kinetic typography, and stylized text effects.

• **Compositing**: Blender's compositing node editor allows for advanced post-processing and effects integration. This is invaluable for enhancing the visual quality of motion graphics.

Workflow in Motion Graphics

Here's a general workflow for creating motion graphics in Blender:

1. **Concept and Storyboarding**: Begin with a clear concept and storyboard that outlines the key elements and animations you want to include in your motion graphic.
2. **Asset Creation**: Create or import the necessary assets, including 3D models, text elements, and any other objects required for your animation.
3. **Animation**: Animate objects, cameras, and text using Blender's animation tools. Keyframes are used to define the

motion and timing of elements.

4. **Particle Effects**: If your motion graphic requires particle effects like smoke or particles, set up and configure particle systems to achieve the desired visual effects.
5. **Physics Simulations**: Integrate physics simulations where needed, such as cloth or fluid simulations, to enhance the realism of your animation.
6. **Text and Typography**: Utilize Blender's text editing capabilities to create animated titles and text elements. Apply text animations and effects as required.
7. **Compositing and Post-Processing**: Use Blender's node-based compositing editor to fine-tune the visual appearance of your motion graphic. Apply color grading, blur effects, and more to enhance the final look.
8. **Rendering**: Render the animation using Blender's rendering engines, such as Eevee or Cycles. Configure output settings, resolution, and frame rate according to your project requirements.
9. **Export and Delivery**: Depending on your intended output, export the motion graphic as a video file or image sequence. You can also export to specific formats suitable for video editing or further post-production.

Typography and Design Principles

Typography is a crucial aspect of motion graphics. Blender provides tools for creating dynamic and visually appealing text animations. Consider the following design principles:

- **Hierarchy**: Use font size, weight, and color to establish a hierarchy of information. Important messages should stand out.

• **Readability**: Ensure that text is easily readable, even during fast-paced animations. Choose legible fonts and use appropriate contrast.

• **Alignment and Positioning**: Align text elements for a clean and organized look. Pay attention to the positioning of text within the composition.

• **Transitions**: Apply smooth transitions and animations to text elements to engage the audience and guide their focus.

Integrating 2D and 3D Elements

Blender allows for the seamless integration of 2D and 3D elements in motion graphics. You can combine 3D models, text, and visual effects with 2D graphics and video footage. This versatility enables creative freedom in designing engaging and dynamic motion graphics.

Successful Motion Graphics Projects

Motion graphics created with Blender can be used in various contexts, including advertisements, title sequences for films and videos, informational videos, and more. Blender's flexibility and powerful toolset make it a valuable choice for motion graphic designers and animators seeking to deliver impactful visual messages.

In conclusion, Blender is a capable and versatile software tool for motion graphics and design. Its animation, particle systems, physics simulations, text editing, and compositing capabilities make it a comprehensive solution for creating visually stunning and engaging motion graphics. Whether you are producing animations for advertising, entertainment, or informational purposes, Blender offers the tools and workflow necessary to bring your creative ideas to life.

14.2 Techniques for Dynamic and Engaging Motion Design

Creating dynamic and engaging motion design in Blender involves combining animation, visual effects, and design principles to convey messages or tell stories effectively. In this section, we will explore techniques and best practices for achieving impactful motion design using Blender.

Storytelling Through Animation

One of the core principles of motion design is storytelling. Effective storytelling helps convey a message or evoke emotions in the audience. Here's how Blender can be used for storytelling in motion design:

- **Storyboarding**: Start with a clear storyboard that outlines the sequence of scenes and key moments in your animation. This helps in visualizing the narrative flow.

- **Character Animation**: If your motion design involves characters, Blender offers a range of tools for character rigging and animation. Use the timeline and keyframes to bring characters to life.

- **Keyframe Animation**: Animate objects, cameras, and characters using keyframes. Blender's graph editor allows for precise control over animation curves and timing.

- **Camera Movements**: Dynamic camera movements can enhance storytelling. Utilize Blender's camera animation capabilities to create compelling shots that guide the viewer's attention.

Visual Effects and Compositing

Visual effects (VFX) play a significant role in motion design, adding visual interest and impact. Blender's compositing and VFX capabilities are valuable for this purpose:

- **Particle Systems**: Blender's particle systems can generate a wide range of effects, from explosions to confetti. These effects can be integrated seamlessly into your animations.

- **Green Screen and Chroma Keying**: If you have footage shot against a green screen, Blender's compositing nodes allow for easy chroma keying and background replacement.

- **Motion Tracking**: Blender includes a motion tracking module that enables you to incorporate 3D elements into live-action footage. This is useful for creating augmented reality effects or integrating animated characters into real environments.

- **Color Grading**: Blender's compositing nodes provide tools for color correction and grading, allowing you to enhance the visual aesthetics of your motion design.

Typography and Kinetic Typography

Text and typography are essential components of motion design. Blender offers features for creating dynamic text animations:

- **Text Effects**: Animate text elements to enter, exit, and transform during your motion design. Blender's animation tools can be used to create kinetic typography.

- **Text Transitions**: Apply smooth transitions to text, enhancing the visual flow of your animation. Use keyframes to control text position, rotation, and scale over time.

- **Dynamic Titles**: Blender's text objects can be easily customized with fonts, colors, and effects. This flexibility allows for the creation of engaging title sequences and informational graphics.

Sound Design and Timing

Sound design is a crucial aspect of motion design, as it complements the visual elements and enhances the viewer's experience:

- **Audio Sync**: Sync your animations with audio cues and dialogue. Blender's timeline and keyframe animation tools make it easy to align visual elements with sound.

- **Sound Effects**: Add sound effects to your motion design to emphasize actions or create atmosphere. Blender's video sequencer can be used to synchronize sound with video.

- **Music Selection**: Choose appropriate music or soundtracks that match the mood and theme of your animation. The right music can greatly enhance the emotional impact of your motion design.

Iteration and Feedback

Iterative design is essential in motion design. Regularly review your work, gather feedback, and make improvements:

- **Feedback Loops**: Share your work with peers, clients, or test audiences to gather feedback on pacing, clarity, and visual appeal.

- **Version Control**: Maintain organized project files with version control to easily track changes and revert to previous iterations if necessary.

- **Continuous Learning**: Stay updated with the latest motion design trends, techniques, and software updates, including new features in Blender.

Export and Delivery

Once your motion design is complete, consider the intended output and delivery format:

- **Video Export**: Export your animation as a video file in a suitable format and resolution. Blender provides various video codecs and settings for customization.

- **Web and Social Media**: Optimize your motion design for online platforms and social media by considering aspect ratios, file sizes, and encoding settings.

- **Interactive Formats**: If your motion design includes interactive elements, such as buttons or links, export it in a format compatible with interactive platforms or websites.

In conclusion, Blender offers a comprehensive set of tools and capabilities for creating dynamic and engaging motion design. By incorporating storytelling, visual effects, typography, sound design, and iterative feedback, you can produce motion design that effectively communicates messages, captivates audiences, and leaves a lasting impression. Whether you're working on animations for marketing, entertainment, education, or other purposes, Blender's versatility makes it a valuable tool for motion designers.

14.3 Integrating 2D and 3D Elements in Motion Graphics

The integration of both 2D and 3D elements is a powerful technique in motion graphics design. Blender provides a versatile environment for seamlessly combining these elements to create engaging and visually striking animations. In this section, we'll explore the techniques and considerations for effectively integrating 2D and 3D elements in Blender motion graphics.

The Power of Integration

Integrating 2D and 3D elements in motion graphics offers several advantages:

• **Enhanced Visual Depth**: By combining 3D objects with 2D graphics, you can create a sense of depth and realism in your animations.

• **Creative Freedom**: The ability to work with both 2D and 3D elements allows for creative freedom and opens up a wide range of design possibilities.

• **Dynamic Interactions**: Interactive elements and animations can be seamlessly incorporated into the visual narrative, engaging the audience more effectively.

Creating 2D Graphics

Before integrating 2D graphics into your Blender motion graphics project, you need to create or prepare the 2D assets:

• **Vector Graphics**: Use vector graphics software like Adobe Illustrator or Inkscape to design your 2D assets. Vector graphics are ideal because they can be easily scaled without losing quality.

• **Raster Graphics**: For certain visual elements, such as textures or photographs, raster graphics created in software like Adobe Photoshop can be used.

• **Transparency**: Utilize transparency in your 2D graphics where needed. Blender supports the use of alpha channels for transparency in both 2D and 3D elements.

Importing and Using 2D Graphics

Once your 2D assets are ready, you can import them into Blender and integrate them into your motion graphics project:

- **Import Formats**: Blender supports various image formats, including PNG, JPEG, and SVG. Import your 2D assets as image planes or textures.

- **Image Planes**: You can add an image plane in Blender and assign your 2D graphic as a texture. This allows you to easily position and manipulate the 2D element in 3D space.

- **Texture Mapping**: Apply your 2D graphics as textures to 3D objects. Blender provides UV mapping tools for accurate texture placement on 3D surfaces.

Camera and Scene Setup

To effectively integrate 2D and 3D elements, careful camera and scene setup are essential:

- **Camera Matching**: Ensure that the camera used for capturing 2D footage matches the camera in your Blender scene. This helps maintain perspective and scale consistency.

- **Layer Organization**: Organize your Blender scene layers to separate 2D and 3D elements. This allows for better control during animation and compositing.

- **Depth of Field**: Consider using depth of field settings in Blender's camera to simulate realistic focus effects and enhance the integration between 2D and 3D elements.

Compositing and Overlays

Blender's compositing node editor is a powerful tool for integrating and blending 2D and 3D elements:

- **Compositing Nodes**: Use nodes to apply various effects, adjust colors, and blend 2D and 3D elements seamlessly. Nodes like "Alpha Over" and "Mix" are commonly used for this purpose.

- **Z-Depth Pass**: Utilize Blender's Z-Depth pass to control the depth-based compositing of 2D and 3D elements. This helps in creating realistic depth-based effects.

- **Object Index Pass**: Assign object index passes to 3D objects to gain precise control over compositing and effects on specific objects.

Visual Consistency

Maintaining visual consistency between 2D and 3D elements is crucial for a polished and professional result:

- **Color Grading**: Apply color grading and correction to both 2D and 3D elements to ensure they match in terms of color balance and tone.

- **Lighting**: Match the lighting conditions in your 3D scene with the lighting in the 2D elements to create a cohesive visual style.

- **Shadows and Reflections**: Consider adding shadows and reflections to 3D objects to make them appear more integrated into the 2D environment.

Rendering and Export

When rendering your motion graphics project, pay attention to rendering settings and output formats:

- **Output Formats**: Choose a suitable output format for your final animation. Blender supports various video formats, including MP4, AVI, and more.

- **Resolution**: Set the resolution of your animation to match the desired output, whether it's for web, broadcast, or high-resolution screens.

- **Export with Transparency**: If needed, configure your rendering settings to export animations with an alpha channel for transparency.

User Interaction

Integrating 2D and 3D elements also opens the door to user interaction in motion graphics:

- **Buttons and Clickable Areas**: Create 2D elements that act as buttons or clickable areas within your 3D scene.

These can trigger animations, transitions, or user interactions.

- **Interactive Storytelling**: Use Blender's logic editor to add interactivity to your motion graphics, allowing users to explore and engage with the content.

In conclusion, integrating 2D and 3D elements in Blender motion graphics projects offers a wide range of creative possibilities. By carefully planning your scene, preparing 2D assets, and using Blender's compositing capabilities, you can achieve seamless integration that enhances the visual depth and impact of your animations. Whether you're creating educational animations, marketing materials, or entertainment content, the combination of 2D and 3D elements can make your motion graphics more engaging and effective.

14.4 Typography and Design Principles in Motion Graphics

Typography plays a fundamental role in motion graphics, as it involves the presentation of text and how it interacts with the visual elements and animation. Effective typography can greatly enhance the overall impact of your motion graphics projects. In this section, we'll delve into typography and design principles specific to motion graphics in Blender.

The Importance of Typography

Typography in motion graphics encompasses the design and animation of text elements, including titles, subtitles, captions, and other textual information. Here are key considerations for typography in motion graphics:

- **Communication**: Text communicates information, context, and messages to the audience. Typography choices should align with the intended message and tone of your animation.

- **Visual Appeal**: Typography should not only be informative but also visually engaging. Well-designed text elements enhance the overall aesthetics of the animation.

- **Clarity**: Text should be easily readable, even during fast-paced animations. The choice of fonts, font sizes, and contrast plays a significant role in readability.

- **Narrative Flow**: Typography can guide the viewer's attention and reinforce the narrative flow of the animation. Proper timing and animation of text elements can help convey the story effectively.

Font Selection

Choosing the right fonts is a crucial step in typography for motion graphics:

- **Font Personality**: Different fonts convey different personalities and emotions. Serif fonts may suggest tradition and formality, while sans-serif fonts often convey modernity and simplicity.

- **Readability**: Prioritize readability when selecting fonts. Avoid overly decorative or complex fonts that may hinder legibility, especially at small sizes or on screens.

- **Consistency**: Maintain font consistency throughout your animation to establish a cohesive visual identity.

Consistent font choices enhance brand recognition and overall aesthetics.

Kinetic Typography

Kinetic typography, also known as text animation, involves animating text elements to create dynamic and engaging visuals. Blender provides various tools for kinetic typography:

- **Keyframing Text**: Animate text elements using keyframes to control their position, scale, rotation, and opacity over time.

- **Text Effects**: Blender's animation tools allow you to apply effects such as fading in, sliding, scaling, and rotating text. These effects can emphasize text and create engaging transitions.

- **Timing**: Consider the timing of text animations in relation to other visual elements and the pacing of your animation. Proper timing ensures that text appears at the right moments to convey information effectively.

Design Principles

Motion graphics in Blender benefit from applying design principles commonly used in graphic design and animation:

- **Hierarchy**: Establish a visual hierarchy with text elements to guide the viewer's attention. Titles should be prominent, and subtitles or captions should be clearly differentiated.

- **Alignment and Composition**: Carefully align and compose text elements within the frame. Utilize grids, guides, and the rule of thirds for balanced compositions.

- **Contrast**: Create contrast between text and background to enhance readability. Adjust text color, font size, and background colors accordingly.

- **Consistency**: Maintain a consistent design language throughout your animation. Consistency in typography, color schemes, and visual style ensures a polished look.

- **Negative Space**: Consider the use of negative space (empty areas) around text to draw attention and reduce visual clutter.

Text Transitions

Text transitions are an effective way to introduce or emphasize textual information in motion graphics:

- **Fade-In/Out**: Gradually fading text elements in and out of the frame is a classic text transition that can be elegant and understated.

- **Motion Transitions**: Use motion to transition between text elements. For example, text can slide, bounce, or rotate into view.

- **Masking**: Employ masking techniques to reveal or conceal text elements. This adds an element of intrigue and surprise.

- **Text Paths**: Animate text along paths to create dynamic and visually engaging transitions. Blender's animation tools allow for precise control over text path animations.

Sound and Typography

Sound design is closely tied to typography in motion graphics:

- **Audio Sync**: Synchronize text animations with audio cues and dialogue. Timing text appearances with relevant audio enhances the viewer's understanding and engagement.

- **Sound Effects**: Consider adding sound effects that complement text animations. For example, text appearing with a subtle sound effect can draw attention.

- **Voiceovers**: If your animation includes voiceovers, ensure that text elements align with the pacing and content of the spoken words.

Export and Delivery

When your motion graphics project involves typography, consider the following for export and delivery:

- **Subtitles and Captions**: If your animation includes subtitles or captions, export your video with embedded or separate subtitle files in commonly supported formats.

- **Font Licensing**: Ensure that the fonts used in your animation are properly licensed and embedded in the final video to avoid font substitution issues.

- **Resolution and Format**: Select an appropriate resolution and video format for your intended delivery platform, whether it's web, broadcast, or cinema.

In summary, typography is a critical element in motion graphics design, and Blender provides the tools and flexibility to create engaging and visually appealing text animations. By carefully considering font selection, kinetic typography, design principles, text transitions, and sound integration, you can effectively convey messages and captivate your audience with text in motion graphics.

14.5 Case Studies: Successful Motion Graphics Projects in Blender

In this section, we'll explore real-world case studies of successful motion graphics projects created using Blender. These examples showcase the versatility of Blender as a powerful tool for creating engaging and impactful motion graphics across various industries and applications.

Case Study 1: Educational Animation

Objective: To create an educational animation for a science museum's interactive exhibit.

Description: A science museum wanted to explain the concept of planetary orbits in a visually engaging way. Blender was used to create a 3D model of the solar system and animate the movement of planets around the sun. Textual explanations and labels were integrated seamlessly with the 3D animation to enhance viewer understanding.

Key Features Used:

- Kinetic typography to display planet names and descriptions.
- 3D modeling and animation for the solar system.
- Realistic lighting and shading to mimic space.

Outcome: The animation effectively conveyed complex scientific concepts to museum visitors, making learning fun and interactive. The use of Blender allowed for dynamic visuals that captivated the audience.

Case Study 2: Marketing Animation

Objective: To create a promotional animation for a new product launch.

Description: A tech company wanted to showcase the features of their latest smartphone in a promotional video. Blender was used to create sleek 3D models of the phone, highlighting its design and functionalities. Kinetic typography and motion graphics were employed to emphasize key features and specifications.

Key Features Used:

- Kinetic typography for feature callouts.
- 3D modeling and animation for the smartphone.
- Realistic material and lighting rendering.

Outcome: The promotional animation generated significant buzz and interest in the new product. Blender's ability to create high-quality 3D visuals contributed to the video's success.

Case Study 3: Music Video

Objective: To produce a visually stunning music video for an independent artist.

Description: An independent musician wanted a visually striking music video for their latest song. Blender was used to create surreal and abstract 3D environments that synchronized with the music. Kinetic typography and text animations were integrated to display lyrics and convey the song's message.

Key Features Used:

- Complex 3D scene creation.
- Audio synchronization for animations.
- Typography animations for lyrics.

Outcome: The music video received acclaim for its unique visuals and the seamless integration of 3D environments with the music. Blender's capabilities allowed for artistic freedom in creating a visually captivating experience.

Case Study 4: Corporate Presentation

Objective: To develop an engaging corporate presentation for an annual conference.

Description: A large corporation needed an attention-grabbing presentation for their annual conference. Blender was used to create 3D animations and infographics that visualized the company's achievements and goals. Kinetic typography and motion graphics were employed to convey key messages effectively.

Key Features Used:

- Infographic animations.
- 3D data visualization.
- Kinetic typography for key points.

Outcome: The corporate presentation was well-received by conference attendees, and it effectively communicated the company's accomplishments and vision. Blender's ability to create dynamic visual elements elevated the presentation.

Case Study 5: Social Media Advertisements

Objective: To produce short, eye-catching social media advertisements.

Description: A small business wanted to create attention-grabbing ads for their products on social media platforms. Blender was used to create short animations that showcased product features and benefits. Kinetic typography and motion graphics were used to highlight key selling points.

Key Features Used:

- Short and impactful animations.
- Kinetic typography for concise messaging.
- Seamless integration of 3D product models.

Outcome: The social media advertisements garnered high engagement and click-through rates. Blender's efficiency in creating quick yet visually appealing animations was instrumental in the campaign's success.

These case studies highlight the diverse range of applications for Blender in motion graphics, from education and marketing to music videos and corporate presentations. Blender's versatility, 3D capabilities, kinetic typography tools, and integration of text and visuals make it a valuable choice for creative professionals in various industries.

15.1 Digital Sculpting in Blender: An Overview

Digital sculpting is a powerful technique in 3D graphics that allows artists to create intricate and detailed 3D models by manipulating digital clay. Blender provides robust digital sculpting capabilities that have become increasingly popular among 3D artists and character designers. In this section, we'll explore the fundamentals of digital sculpting in Blender and its applications in various creative projects.

Understanding Digital Sculpting

Digital sculpting is a technique that simulates the process of traditional sculpture but in a digital environment. It allows artists to use virtual tools to shape and mold digital clay, creating intricate 3D models with fine details and organic shapes. Blender's sculpting tools provide artists with a versatile and intuitive way to bring their creative visions to life.

Sculpt Mode in Blender

Blender's Sculpt Mode is the primary workspace for digital sculpting. Here's an overview of essential features and tools within Sculpt Mode:

- **Brushes**: Blender offers a variety of sculpting brushes, each designed for specific tasks such as adding, smoothing, or carving details. Artists can customize brushes to suit their needs.

- **Dynamic Topology**: Blender's sculpting mode supports dynamic topology, allowing the software to automatically adapt the mesh's resolution as artists sculpt. This enables artists to focus on creating without worrying about topology constraints.

• **Multi-Resolution Sculpting**: Artists can work with multiple levels of detail, which is especially useful for refining details on specific parts of a model.

• **Symmetry**: Symmetry tools enable artists to sculpt symmetrically, which is essential for character design and organic modeling.

• **Texture Painting**: Blender allows artists to paint directly onto their sculpts, enabling the addition of intricate textures and fine details.

Sculpting Workflow

The digital sculpting workflow in Blender typically follows these steps:

1. **Base Mesh**: Start with a basic 3D model that serves as the foundation for your sculpt. This can be a primitive shape or a low-poly model.
2. **Sculpting**: Enter Sculpt Mode and begin sculpting by selecting brushes and using them to manipulate the mesh. Focus on defining the overall shape and adding major details first.
3. **Dynamic Topology**: As you refine your sculpt, Blender's dynamic topology will automatically adjust the mesh's resolution to capture finer details.
4. **Multi-Resolution**: If needed, use multi-resolution levels to switch between lower and higher detail versions of your

sculpt. This allows for efficient detailing.

5. **Texture Painting**: Add texture details to your sculpt using Blender's texture painting tools. You can paint color, displacement, bump, and other texture maps directly onto the model.
6. **Retopology**: Depending on your project, you may need to perform retopology to create a clean and optimized mesh suitable for animation or rendering.
7. **Materials and Rendering**: Apply materials and set up lighting and rendering to showcase your sculpt in its best form.

Applications of Digital Sculpting in Blender

Digital sculpting in Blender finds applications in various creative fields, including:

- **Character Design**: Digital sculpting is widely used in character design for video games, animation, and films. Artists can create lifelike characters with intricate facial expressions and details.

- **Creature Design**: Creature designers use sculpting to create fantastical creatures and monsters, exploring unique and imaginative forms.

- **Props and Environment**: Sculpting extends to props, objects, and environmental assets. Artists can craft detailed props and scenery elements for diverse settings.

- **Concept Art**: Sculpting in Blender aids concept artists in exploring and visualizing ideas for characters, creatures, and environments.

- **3D Printing**: Artists can use Blender's sculpting tools to design 3D-printed sculptures and prototypes. The level of detail achievable through digital sculpting enhances the quality of printed objects.

- **Artistic Exploration**: Digital sculpting provides artists with a platform to experiment and push creative boundaries, leading to unique and innovative art pieces.

Sculpting Tips

To excel in digital sculpting with Blender, consider these tips:

- **Practice**: Like any artistic skill, practice is crucial. Regularly sculpting will improve your proficiency and creativity.

- **Study Anatomy**: If you're sculpting characters, a strong understanding of anatomy is essential for creating realistic figures.

- **Reference Images**: Use reference images or anatomical references to guide your sculpting, especially for accurate representation.

- **Experiment**: Don't be afraid to experiment with different brushes, settings, and techniques. Blender's sculpting tools offer plenty of room for exploration.

- **Iterate**: Sculpting is an iterative process. Be prepared to make changes, refine details, and iterate on your work.

Digital sculpting in Blender opens up a world of creative possibilities, allowing artists to bring their visions to life with incredible detail and precision. Whether you're sculpting characters, creatures, or intricate props, Blender's sculpting tools provide a versatile and accessible platform for artistic expression.

15.2 Tools and Techniques for Effective Sculpting

Digital sculpting in Blender is a versatile and creative process, and understanding the available tools and techniques is crucial for achieving your artistic goals. In this section, we'll delve into some of the essential tools and techniques that can help you become a proficient digital sculptor in Blender.

Sculpting Brushes

Blender provides a wide range of sculpting brushes, each tailored to specific tasks. Here are some commonly used sculpting brushes and their functions:

- **Draw Brush**: The Draw brush is the default brush for sculpting. It allows you to add material to your model, building up forms and details.

- **Smooth Brush**: The Smooth brush is used to smooth out surfaces and reduce the appearance of roughness or bumps. It's essential for achieving a polished look in your sculpts.

- **Clay Strips Brush**: This brush is great for adding material quickly, making it useful for blocking out forms and adding bulk to your sculptures.

- **Crease Brush**: The Crease brush is designed to create sharp edges and creases in your model. It's handy for defining folds, wrinkles, or hard surface details.

- **Inflate Brush**: The Inflate brush can be used to puff up areas of your sculpt, giving them volume. It's useful for adding a sense of thickness or roundness to certain parts.

- **Grab Brush**: The Grab brush allows you to pull, push, and move parts of your sculpt as if you were physically manipulating clay. It's great for overall shape adjustments.

- **Mask Brush**: The Mask brush lets you paint areas of your model to protect them from sculpting changes. It's useful for focusing on specific areas without affecting the rest of the model.

- **Layer Brush**: This brush allows you to add material in layers, making it easier to control the buildup of details and forms.

Brush Settings

Understanding and customizing brush settings can significantly enhance your sculpting experience. Here are some important brush settings to consider:

- **Brush Strength**: Adjust the strength of your brush's effect. Lower values result in more subtle changes, while higher values have a more pronounced impact.

- **Radius**: Control the size of your brush. You can change the brush size interactively by pressing the 'F' key and dragging the mouse.

- **Auto Smooth**: Enable Auto Smooth to automatically smooth the sculpted surface as you work. This can help maintain a cleaner and more polished appearance.

- **Symmetry**: If you're working on a symmetrical object like a character, enable symmetry to sculpt on both sides simultaneously. Blender's symmetry tools are powerful for maintaining balance.

- **Dynamic Topology**: Dynamic Topology is a crucial setting that adjusts the mesh resolution as you sculpt. It ensures that you have enough detail where you need it without unnecessarily increasing the mesh's complexity.

Detailing Techniques

Achieving fine details is often a primary goal in digital sculpting. Here are some techniques to help you add intricate details to your sculpts:

- **Subdivision Levels**: Use multi-resolution levels to work on different levels of detail. Start with a low-poly base and gradually add more detail as you move up through levels.

- **Brush Strength Variation**: Vary the strength of your brush strokes to create natural variations in texture and detail. Lighter strokes can add subtlety, while stronger strokes define major features.

- **Alpha Textures**: Blender allows you to use alpha textures with your brushes. These textures can add complex patterns, scales, or textures to your sculpt.

- **Layering Brushes**: Layer different brushes and techniques to build up complexity and depth in your sculpt. For example, you can start with broad strokes using the Clay Strips brush and then refine with finer brushes like the Crease brush.

Reference and Anatomy

When sculpting realistic characters or objects, having references and an understanding of anatomy is essential. Use reference images, anatomy books, or even 3D models as guides for your work. Pay close attention to proportions, muscle structure, and surface details to achieve a lifelike result.

Practicing and Iterating

Digital sculpting is an art form that improves with practice. Don't be discouraged by early attempts; instead, embrace them as learning experiences. Sculpting allows for a great deal of experimentation, so don't hesitate to iterate and refine your work as you go along.

Performance Considerations

Sculpting in high-resolution or with many dynamic topology changes can be demanding on your computer's resources. If you experience performance issues, consider using simplified proxy meshes or hiding parts of your model that you're not currently working on to optimize your workflow.

In summary, mastering digital sculpting in Blender involves familiarizing yourself with the available brushes, customizing brush settings, and employing various detailing techniques. It's also crucial to use references and practice regularly to refine your skills. Whether you're sculpting characters, creatures, or objects, Blender's sculpting tools provide a dynamic and versatile platform for your creative expression.

15.3 Creating Artistic and Stylized Models

Digital sculpting in Blender isn't limited to realism; it's also a powerful tool for creating artistic and stylized 3D models. Whether you want to craft characters with exaggerated features, explore abstract forms, or create sculptures with a unique artistic flair, Blender's sculpting tools provide the flexibility to bring your creative vision to life. In this section, we'll explore techniques and considerations for crafting artistic and stylized models.

Embrace Artistic Freedom

One of the key advantages of digital sculpting is the freedom it offers artists to experiment and push the boundaries of traditional sculpting. You're not bound by the limitations of physical materials, allowing you to create forms and shapes that are impossible in reality. Embrace this artistic freedom to explore new ideas and concepts.

Reference and Inspiration

Even when pursuing a stylized or abstract approach, references and inspiration can be invaluable. They can help you grasp fundamental shapes, proportions, and anatomical elements that you can then manipulate and exaggerate in your stylized work. Consider collecting reference images, sketches, or other artwork that resonates with your vision.

Exaggeration and Distortion

Artistic and stylized models often involve exaggeration and distortion of proportions and features. For characters, you might elongate limbs, enlarge eyes, or emphasize certain facial features to convey specific personalities or emotions. Experiment with different levels of exaggeration to find a style that suits your vision.

Expressive Sculpting

Stylized models often prioritize expressiveness over realism. Focus on creating dynamic poses, lively facial expressions, and exaggerated gestures. These elements can imbue your models with character and personality, making them more engaging and memorable.

Texture and Detail

Even in stylized models, texture and detail play essential roles. Consider the surface treatment of your models. You can use brushes to add texture, patterns, or unique surface treatments that enhance the stylized look. Experiment with different brushes and techniques to achieve the desired artistic effect.

Silhouettes and Flow

Pay attention to the overall silhouette and flow of your models. Silhouettes should be distinctive and instantly recognizable. Consider how the lines and curves of your model's form interact to create a harmonious flow. A well-designed silhouette can make your model stand out and convey a strong visual identity.

Color and Material

While digital sculpting primarily focuses on form and shape, color and material choices can greatly influence the stylized look. Experiment with vibrant color schemes, non-realistic materials, and shader effects to enhance the artistic qualities of your models. Blender's material and rendering capabilities provide ample room for creative exploration.

Iteration and Feedback

Creating artistic and stylized models often involves a process of iteration and refinement. Don't be afraid to revisit your work multiple times, making adjustments and refinements along the way. Seeking feedback from peers or the Blender community can provide valuable insights and help you refine your artistic style.

Stylized Workflows

Consider establishing workflows and techniques that align with your artistic goals. This might involve creating custom brushes, setting up specific sculpting environments, or using Blender's symmetry and mirroring tools to ensure consistency in your stylized models.

Experiment and Explore

Above all, the creation of artistic and stylized models in Blender is an opportunity for artistic exploration and experimentation. Allow yourself the freedom to take risks, break conventions, and discover new approaches to sculpting. Stylized work often thrives on innovation and pushing the boundaries of traditional aesthetics.

In conclusion, Blender's digital sculpting capabilities provide a versatile platform for creating artistic and stylized 3D models. By embracing artistic freedom, referencing inspiration, using exaggeration and distortion, focusing on expressiveness, considering texture and detail, and experimenting with color and materials, you can craft unique and captivating stylized models that showcase your creative vision and artistic prowess.

15.4 Integrating Sculpting into Your Workflow

Digital sculpting in Blender is a powerful and creative process, and incorporating it effectively into your workflow can greatly enhance your 3D modeling and design projects. In this section, we'll explore how to seamlessly integrate sculpting into your workflow, whether you're creating characters, props, or complex environments.

Establish Clear Objectives

Before you begin sculpting, it's crucial to have clear objectives for your project. What are you trying to achieve with your sculpt? Are you creating a highly detailed character, a stylized object, or a realistic environment? Define your goals, style, and level of detail you want to achieve. Having a clear vision will guide your sculpting process.

Choose the Right Starting Point

Sculpting can be integrated at various stages of your 3D modeling workflow. Consider the following starting points:

- **From a Primitive**: You can start sculpting from a simple primitive shape, such as a sphere or cube, and gradually refine it into your desired model.

- **Low-Poly Base**: Begin with a low-poly base mesh that you've modeled using traditional modeling techniques. Sculpting can then be used to add fine details, wrinkles, or organic shapes.

- **High-Poly Sculpt**: In some cases, you may want to create a high-poly sculpt as the final result, especially for detailed character models or props. In such cases, you can skip the low-poly base and focus on sculpting directly.

Blocking and Refining

Sculpting is not just about adding fine details; it's also about blocking out major forms and refining the overall shape. Start with broad strokes to establish the primary structure of your model. Once you're satisfied with the proportions and major forms, move on to finer details and surface textures.

Sculpting Levels

Blender offers multi-resolution sculpting, allowing you to work at different levels of detail. As you progress, you can switch between these levels to work on broader forms and finer details separately. This approach helps maintain a manageable mesh while achieving high-quality results.

Combining Sculpting with Traditional Modeling

Sculpting can be seamlessly integrated with traditional polygon modeling. For example, you can sculpt intricate character faces while using traditional modeling for clothing or hard surface elements. Blender's sculpt-to-retopology workflows allow you to create a clean, optimized mesh for animation or rendering after sculpting.

Retopology

Depending on your project's requirements, you may need to perform retopology. This process involves creating a clean and optimized topology for your sculpted model. Retopologized models are suitable for animation, rigging, and rendering. Blender provides retopology tools and addons to simplify this step.

Texture Painting

After sculpting, you can also incorporate texture painting to add color, surface details, and textures to your model. Blender's texture painting tools allow you to paint directly on your sculpt and create realistic or stylized textures.

Rigging and Animation

If your project involves character modeling, sculpted characters can be rigged and animated for various purposes. Blender's rigging tools and animation capabilities make it possible to bring your sculpted characters to life.

Export and Rendering

Once your sculpted model is complete, you can export it for use in other software or render it directly in Blender. Pay attention to render settings, materials, and lighting to achieve the desired final look.

Backup and Version Control

As with any creative process, it's essential to maintain backups and version control of your work. Blender provides features for saving multiple versions of your project, which can be helpful when experimenting with different sculpting approaches.

Incorporating digital sculpting into your 3D modeling workflow in Blender offers endless creative possibilities. Whether you're sculpting characters, props, or environments, defining clear objectives, choosing the right starting point, and seamlessly combining sculpting with traditional modeling are key steps in creating compelling 3D models. Remember to adapt your workflow to suit your project's specific requirements and continuously refine your skills through practice and experimentation.

15.5 Exploring Artistic Possibilities with Blender Sculpting

Blender's sculpting capabilities offer a wide range of artistic possibilities for 3D artists and designers. In this section, we'll delve into some advanced and creative techniques to help you explore the full potential of sculpting in Blender.

Custom Brushes

While Blender provides a variety of sculpting brushes by default, creating custom brushes can elevate your sculpting game. Custom brushes allow you to achieve unique textures, patterns, and effects. To create a custom brush, you can sculpt a shape or texture on a plane, save it as an image, and then use it as a brush texture. Experiment with different brush shapes and textures to add intricate details to your sculpts.

Dynamic Topology

Dynamic Topology is a powerful feature in Blender sculpting that dynamically adjusts the mesh's topology as you sculpt. This means you can add or remove detail where needed, rather than being limited by the initial mesh resolution. It's particularly useful when sculpting organic forms or highly detailed models. To enable Dynamic Topology, go to the Sculpting workspace, open the Dyntopo panel, and adjust the Detail Refine Method and Detail Size settings to control the level of detail.

Sculpting with Symmetry

Blender offers symmetry tools that allow you to sculpt on both sides of your model simultaneously. This feature is incredibly helpful for maintaining symmetry in character modeling or creating symmetrical objects. To enable symmetry, go to the Symmetry section in the Brush panel and choose the axis of symmetry that suits your model.

Layering and Masking

Layering different sculpting techniques and using masks can add depth and complexity to your sculpts. You can use the Mask Brush to protect certain areas of your model from sculpting changes while focusing on specific regions. Additionally, you can use the Layer Brush to add material in layers, building up details gradually for a more controlled sculpting process.

Incorporating Blender's Other Tools

Sculpting doesn't have to be isolated from Blender's other tools and functionalities. You can seamlessly integrate sculpting into your 3D modeling workflow by combining it with traditional polygon modeling, retopology, UV mapping, and more. For example, after sculpting a character's face, you can use traditional modeling techniques to create clothing or accessories, then perform retopology for animation purposes.

Texture Painting and Materials

Texture painting in Blender allows you to add color, surface details, and textures to your sculpts. You can paint directly on your sculpted model, creating realistic or stylized textures. Additionally, Blender's material and shader capabilities enable you to experiment with a wide range of surface materials, from metals and plastics to skin and fur.

Experimentation and Creativity

The true essence of sculpting in Blender lies in experimentation and creativity. Don't be afraid to push the boundaries, take risks, and explore new artistic directions. Sculpting is an organic and intuitive process that rewards artistic innovation. You can use it to create fantastical creatures, abstract art, intricate characters, and much more.

Practice and Learning

As with any artistic skill, practice is key to mastering Blender sculpting. The more you sculpt, the better you'll become at manipulating forms, understanding anatomy, and achieving the desired results. Learning from tutorials, books, and the Blender community can also provide valuable insights and techniques to improve your sculpting skills.

Sharing and Collaborating

Blender's open-source nature encourages sharing and collaboration. You can share your sculpting work with the Blender community, contribute to open-source projects, or collaborate with other artists on creative endeavors. Engaging with the community can lead to valuable feedback, inspiration, and opportunities for growth.

In summary, Blender's sculpting capabilities offer limitless artistic possibilities. By exploring custom brushes, using Dynamic Topology, sculpting with symmetry, layering and masking, incorporating other Blender tools, texture painting, and embracing experimentation and creativity, you can unlock the full potential of Blender sculpting. Remember that practice, learning, and collaboration are essential elements of sculpting mastery, so don't hesitate to dive into this exciting world of digital artistry.

Chapter 16: Real-Time Rendering and VR

16.1 Exploring Real-Time Rendering in Blender

In this section, we will delve into the exciting realm of real-time rendering using Blender. Real-time rendering is a crucial aspect of 3D graphics, particularly in the context of virtual reality (VR) and interactive experiences. Blender has made significant strides in this domain, and understanding its capabilities can open up a world of possibilities for creating immersive and interactive content.

Understanding Real-Time Rendering

Real-time rendering refers to the process of generating and displaying 3D graphics in real-time, allowing for immediate interaction and feedback. Unlike traditional offline rendering, where frames are generated sequentially and can take hours or even days to complete, real-time rendering aims to produce images or animations on-the-fly, often at 30 frames per second (FPS) or more.

Blender excels in real-time rendering thanks to its powerful game engine and integration with real-time technologies like Eevee. Eevee is a real-time PBR (Physically-Based Rendering) engine that provides stunning results with minimal rendering times. It's well-suited for creating VR experiences and interactive 3D content.

Setting up Real-Time Projects

Before you start diving into real-time rendering with Blender, you need to set up your projects properly. Here are some key considerations:

1. **Asset Optimization**: Real-time rendering demands optimized 3D models and textures to ensure smooth performance. Reduce polygon counts, use efficient texture maps, and consider level of detail (LOD) techniques.
2. **Physics and Interactivity**: Think about the interactive elements of your scene. Will there be physics simulations, user interactions, or dynamic lighting? Blender offers tools for physics simulations like rigid bodies, soft bodies, and fluids.
3. **VR Integration**: If your goal is to create VR content, you'll need to ensure compatibility with VR headsets. Blender has built-in support for various VR devices and platforms.

Utilizing Eevee for Real-Time Rendering

Blender's Eevee engine is at the forefront of real-time rendering. Here's how you can leverage its capabilities:

```
# Enable Eevee in Blender's Render Engine settings

import bpy

bpy.context.scene.render.engine = 'BLENDER_EEVEE'
```

Eevee supports features like:

- **PBR Materials**: Use physically-based materials to achieve realistic reflections, refractions, and shading.

- **Real-Time Shadows**: Eevee provides real-time shadow mapping for dynamic scenes.

- **Screen-Space Reflections (SSR)**: Achieve accurate reflections even in complex scenes.

• **Bloom and Depth of Field**: Enhance the visual appeal of your scenes with post-processing effects.

Optimizing for Performance

Real-time rendering requires efficient performance optimization. Here are some tips:

• **Level of Detail (LOD)**: Implement LOD systems to reduce the complexity of distant objects.

• **Texture Streaming**: Use texture streaming techniques to load textures dynamically based on the camera's position.

• **Batching**: Combine multiple objects into a single mesh to reduce draw calls.

• **Culling**: Implement frustum and occlusion culling techniques to avoid rendering unseen objects.

Conclusion

Real-time rendering in Blender, especially with the Eevee engine, opens up exciting possibilities for creating interactive 3D content and virtual reality experiences. Understanding the fundamentals of real-time rendering, project setup, and optimization is key to achieving stunning results in this dynamic field. As we continue through this chapter, we'll explore more advanced techniques and applications for real-time rendering and VR in Blender.

16.2 Blender and Virtual Reality: Creating Immersive Experiences

Virtual reality (VR) is a transformative technology that has revolutionized how we experience digital content. In this section, we'll explore how Blender can be used to create immersive VR experiences. VR allows users to step into a virtual world, making it an ideal platform for games, simulations, training, and interactive storytelling.

Understanding VR in Blender

Blender offers robust support for VR content creation, allowing you to develop VR applications and experiences with ease. To get started, you'll need compatible VR hardware, such as VR headsets and motion controllers. Blender supports various VR platforms, including Oculus Rift, HTC Vive, and Windows Mixed Reality.

Setting up Blender for VR

Before diving into VR content creation, you need to set up Blender for VR development. Follow these steps to get started:

1. **Install VR Hardware and Software**: Ensure you have the necessary VR hardware (headset and controllers) and VR software (e.g., SteamVR) installed and configured on your computer.
2. **Enable VR Support in Blender**: In Blender, navigate to the Preferences menu, and under the Add-ons tab, search for "VR" or "Virtual Reality." Enable the VR add-on that corresponds to your VR hardware.
3. **Configure VR Settings**: Go to the Scene settings in Blender, and you'll find a "Virtual Reality" section. Here, you can select your VR headset and controllers and

configure tracking and input settings.

4. **Create a VR-Friendly Scene**: When designing a VR experience, consider factors like scale and interactivity. Ensure that the scene is comfortable for users and optimized for performance.

Designing VR Experiences

Creating VR content in Blender involves designing 3D environments, objects, and interactions that users can engage with in virtual space. Here are some key considerations:

- **Immersive Environments**: Design environments that transport users to different worlds, whether it's a fantasy realm, a historical setting, or a futuristic space station.

- **Interactivity**: VR experiences thrive on interactivity. Incorporate interactive elements like picking up objects, pressing buttons, or solving puzzles.

- **Optimization**: Optimize your VR scenes for smooth performance. Use efficient 3D models, textures, and lighting to maintain a high frame rate.

- **User Comfort**: Pay attention to user comfort and prevent motion sickness. Implement techniques like teleportation, smooth locomotion, or snap turning to reduce discomfort.

Testing and Debugging

Testing is a crucial part of VR development. Blender provides tools for testing VR experiences directly within the software. You can enter VR mode to interact with your scene using your VR headset and controllers. This allows you to identify issues, adjust scale, and fine-tune interactions.

```
# Entering VR mode in Blender

import bpy

bpy.ops.wm.xr_session('INVOKE_DEFAULT')
```

Exporting and Sharing VR Content

Once your VR experience is complete, you'll need to export it for your target VR platform. Blender provides export options for various platforms, including Unity and Unreal Engine. You can also export to web-based VR platforms using technologies like WebVR or WebXR.

Conclusion

Blender's support for virtual reality opens up exciting opportunities for creating immersive and interactive experiences. Whether you're developing VR games, architectural walkthroughs, or educational simulations, Blender provides the tools you need to bring your ideas to life in the world of virtual reality. As VR technology continues to evolve, Blender remains a versatile and powerful tool for VR content creators.

16.3 Techniques for Optimizing Real-Time Performance

Optimizing real-time performance is essential when creating VR experiences or interactive content in Blender. Ensuring a smooth and responsive user experience is key to the success of any VR project. In this section, we'll explore various techniques for optimizing real-time performance in Blender.

Efficient Modeling and Texturing

Efficiency starts with the 3D models and textures you use in your VR scenes. Here are some tips for optimizing your assets:

- **Polycount Reduction**: Use simplified geometry for objects that are distant or less important in the scene. High-poly models can be taxing on performance.

- **Texture Optimization**: Keep texture resolutions reasonable, and use compression formats suitable for real-time rendering, such as PBR textures (Albedo, Normal, Roughness, Metallic).

- **UV Mapping**: Efficient UV mapping can reduce texture distortion and improve rendering speed. Consider using tiled textures for large surfaces.

LOD (Level of Detail) Techniques

Level of Detail (LOD) techniques are essential for maintaining performance in VR. LOD involves using different versions of an object with varying levels of detail based on the object's distance from the viewer. Here's how to implement LOD in Blender:

```
# Creating LOD levels in Blender

import bpy

# Create the high-poly object

high_poly_object = bpy.data.objects.new("HighPolyObject", None)
```

```
bpy.context.scene.collection.objects.link(high_poly_object)

# Create a simplified low-poly version

low_poly_object = bpy.data.objects.new("LowPolyObject", None)

bpy.context.scene.collection.objects.link(low_poly_object)

# Set up LOD distances

high_poly_object.lod.distance = 10.0 # High-poly visible up to 10 units

low_poly_object.lod.distance = 50.0 # Low-poly visible beyond 50 units

# Configure LOD for the camera

bpy.data.cameras[0].lod.object = high_poly_object
```

Occlusion Culling

Occlusion culling is a technique used to reduce rendering overhead by avoiding the rendering of objects that are not visible to the camera. Blender provides options for occlusion culling:

- **Frustum Culling**: Blender automatically performs frustum culling, which means objects outside the camera's field of view are not rendered.
- **Occlusion Culling Add-ons**: Some add-ons in Blender can assist with occlusion culling, helping you optimize complex scenes further.

Use Efficient Shading and Lighting

Real-time rendering relies on efficient shading and lighting techniques. Here are some considerations:

- **PBR Materials**: Physically-Based Rendering (PBR) materials offer realistic shading while maintaining performance. Use them for a balanced visual appeal.

- **Light Probes**: Implement light probes for global illumination and reflections. They can improve lighting quality without a significant performance hit.

- **Baking**: Pre-baking lighting and shadows can reduce the computational load during runtime. Blender provides tools for baking various types of textures.

Profiling and Testing

Profiling your VR project is crucial for identifying performance bottlenecks. Blender offers profiling tools to help you diagnose and optimize your scenes:

- **Blender's Profiler**: Use Blender's built-in profiler to analyze the performance of your VR scene, identify areas that need improvement, and track frame rates.

Conclusion

Optimizing real-time performance in Blender is vital for delivering smooth and immersive VR experiences. By efficiently managing 3D assets, implementing LOD techniques, utilizing occlusion culling, and optimizing shading and lighting, you can create VR content that runs smoothly on a variety of hardware configurations. Remember that performance optimization is an iterative process, and continuous testing and profiling will help you fine-tune your VR projects for the best user experience.

16.4 Interactive Design and Real-Time Visualization

Interactive design and real-time visualization are key aspects of creating engaging and immersive VR experiences in Blender. In this section, we'll explore how to design interactive content and leverage real-time visualization techniques to enhance your VR projects.

Importance of Interactivity

Interactivity is a hallmark of VR experiences. It allows users to engage with the virtual world, making them active participants rather than passive observers. Here are some reasons why interactivity is essential:

- **User Engagement**: Interactivity captivates users and keeps them engaged, making the experience more memorable.

- **Learning and Training**: Interactive VR is valuable for educational and training applications, enabling users to practice and learn in a safe and controlled environment.

- **Gameplay**: If you're creating VR games, interactivity is at the core of gameplay mechanics and player enjoyment.

Creating Interactive Elements

Blender provides tools for creating interactive elements in VR scenes. Here's how you can get started:

- **Physics Simulation**: Use Blender's physics simulation capabilities to add realistic interactions. For example, you can simulate objects falling, bouncing, or responding to user input.

- **Rigging and Animation**: Rig characters and objects to respond to user input or trigger animations based on user actions.

- **Scripting**: Write Python scripts to add custom interactivity. For instance, you can create scripts that respond to button presses on VR controllers.

User Interface (UI) Design

Designing an intuitive and user-friendly interface is crucial for VR applications. Consider the following UI design principles:

- **Immersive HUD**: Create UI elements that blend seamlessly with the virtual environment, avoiding elements that appear as overlays.

- **Gaze-Based Interaction**: Implement gaze-based interaction, where users can select options or objects by looking at them and using VR controllers.

- **Hand Tracking**: Utilize hand tracking technology if available to allow users to interact with objects using natural hand movements.

- **Feedback**: Provide visual and haptic feedback to users to acknowledge their interactions and actions.

Real-Time Visualization

Real-time visualization is the ability to see changes in the VR scene as they occur. Blender excels in real-time visualization, especially with the Eevee rendering engine. Here's how to utilize it:

```
# Enable real-time rendering with Eevee

import bpy

bpy.context.scene.render.engine = 'BLENDER_EEVEE'
```

- **Instant Feedback**: With real-time visualization, changes you make to the scene are immediately reflected in the VR environment, allowing for quick iterations and adjustments.
- **Lighting and Shading**: Eevee provides real-time lighting and shading, enabling you to fine-tune the visual aspects of your VR scene.
- **Previewing Interactions**: Real-time visualization allows you to preview how interactive elements will behave in the VR environment, helping you refine interactions.

Conclusion

Interactive design and real-time visualization are essential components of creating immersive and engaging VR experiences in Blender. By understanding the principles of interactivity, designing intuitive user interfaces, and leveraging real-time visualization with Eevee, you can craft VR content that captivates users and provides them with memorable and interactive journeys in virtual worlds. As you continue to develop your VR projects, keep user engagement and interaction at the forefront of your design considerations.

16.5 Future of Real-Time Rendering and VR in Blender

The future of real-time rendering and virtual reality (VR) in Blender holds tremendous promise and potential. As technology continues to advance, Blender evolves to keep pace with emerging trends and technologies. In this section, we'll explore the exciting developments and possibilities that lie ahead for real-time rendering and VR in Blender.

Advancements in Real-Time Rendering

Blender's real-time rendering capabilities are expected to advance in several key areas:

- **Ray Tracing**: Real-time ray tracing, which simulates the behavior of light accurately, is becoming increasingly feasible for real-time rendering. Future Blender versions may integrate ray tracing for even more realistic visuals.

- **Hardware Acceleration**: As graphics hardware continues to evolve, Blender is likely to leverage GPU acceleration for real-time rendering, allowing for faster and more complex scenes.

- **Real-Time AI**: Integration of artificial intelligence (AI) and machine learning could enable features like automated scene optimization, improved anti-aliasing, and more realistic simulations in real-time.

- **Cross-Platform Compatibility**: Blender is likely to expand its support for various VR platforms and headsets, making it easier for developers to create content for a wide audience.

Enhanced VR Development Tools

The future of VR development in Blender will bring enhancements to the VR authoring process:

- **VR Prototyping**: More intuitive tools for quickly prototyping VR experiences within Blender, allowing developers to experiment and iterate rapidly.

- **Simplified Interactivity**: Streamlined methods for adding interactivity to VR scenes, making it easier for creators to design immersive experiences without extensive coding.

- **Collaboration Features**: Improved collaboration features that facilitate teamwork among VR developers, enabling seamless remote collaboration on VR projects.

- **VR-Ready Asset Libraries**: Extensive libraries of VR-ready assets, from 3D models to interactive elements, accessible directly within Blender, simplifying content creation.

Integration with Emerging Technologies

Blender's versatility and open-source nature position it well to integrate with emerging technologies:

- **AR (Augmented Reality)**: Blender may expand its capabilities to support AR development, enabling creators to develop applications that blend digital content with the real world.

- **Blockchain and NFTs**: Integration with blockchain and NFT technologies for asset management and trading within the Blender ecosystem.

- **WebVR and WebXR**: Increased support for WebVR and WebXR, making it easier to create and share VR experiences directly on the web.

- **Immersive Learning**: Blender may play a significant role in the future of immersive learning, with applications in education, training, and virtual museums.

Community and Collaboration

The Blender community is known for its dedication and active collaboration. The future of real-time rendering and VR in Blender will continue to benefit from community contributions:

- **Open-Source Development**: The open-source nature of Blender ensures that new features and improvements are developed transparently and collaboratively by a global community of contributors.

- **Add-ons and Plugins**: A growing ecosystem of add-ons and plugins will extend Blender's VR capabilities, allowing developers to customize and enhance their workflows.

- **Tutorials and Resources**: An abundance of tutorials and learning resources will continue to emerge, helping artists and developers master VR creation in Blender.

Conclusion

The future of real-time rendering and VR in Blender is bright and full of exciting possibilities. With advancements in real-time rendering, enhanced VR development tools, integration with emerging technologies, and a vibrant and collaborative community, Blender remains at the forefront of VR content creation. As VR adoption continues to grow and technology evolves, Blender will play an increasingly pivotal role in empowering creators to bring their virtual worlds to life. It's an exciting time to be a part of the Blender community and explore the limitless potential of real-time rendering and VR.

Chapter 17: Environmental Design and World Building

17.1 Crafting Natural Environments in Blender

Creating natural environments in Blender is a fundamental skill for 3D artists and game developers. Whether you're designing a lush forest, a serene mountain range, or an alien world, Blender provides the tools and techniques you need to bring these environments to life. In this section, we'll explore the art of crafting natural and believable environments using Blender's powerful features.

Understanding Natural Environments

Natural environments are complex and diverse, often characterized by various elements like terrain, vegetation, water bodies, and weather. To recreate them convincingly in Blender, you need to study and understand the following aspects:

- **Reference Materials**: Collect reference images and resources to gain insights into the environment you want to create. Observation and research are crucial.

- **Ecosystems**: Understand the ecological relationships within the environment. How do different elements interact? What species of plants and animals are present?

- **Topography**: Analyze the terrain and landscape. Consider the elevation, terrain features, and geological elements that define the environment.

- **Climate and Weather**: Climate influences the appearance of an environment. Weather conditions like rain, snow, and wind can add realism.

Terrain Modeling

Blender offers various tools for terrain modeling:

- **Heightmaps**: You can import or generate heightmaps to create realistic terrains. Use the Displace modifier to deform a plane's geometry based on a heightmap.

- **Sculpting**: Blender's sculpting tools allow you to shape terrains organically. Sculpt brushes like "Smooth," "Inflate," and "Flatten" are useful for terrain design.

```
# Using sculpting in Blender

import bpy

# Select the terrain object

terrain = bpy.data.objects['Terrain']

# Enter Sculpt Mode

bpy.context.view_layer.objects.active = terrain

bpy.ops.sculpt.sculptmode_toggle()

# Select a sculpt brush

bpy.ops.sculpt.brush_stroke(stroke='SMOOTH')
```

Vegetation and Ecosystems

Adding vegetation is essential for natural environments:

- **Asset Libraries**: Utilize vegetation asset libraries, which include 3D models of plants, trees, and foliage.

- **Particle Systems**: Blender's particle systems allow you to distribute vegetation across the terrain. You can control density, scale, and rotation for realistic results.

- **Ecosystem Simulation**: For more advanced projects, consider simulating ecosystems using Blender's physics capabilities. Implement interactions between plants and animals.

Realistic Materials and Textures

Realistic materials and textures contribute to the authenticity of natural environments:

- **PBR Materials**: Use Physically-Based Rendering (PBR) materials to achieve realistic surface properties like reflectivity, roughness, and color.

- **Texture Painting**: Blender's texture painting tools enable you to create custom textures for terrain, rocks, and other elements.

- **Normal and Displacement Maps**: Apply normal and displacement maps to add fine details to surfaces, such as bumpiness and small-scale imperfections.

Lighting and Atmosphere

Lighting and atmosphere play a crucial role in creating the right mood for your environment:

- **HDR Lighting**: Utilize High Dynamic Range (HDR) images for realistic lighting. HDRIs provide accurate lighting conditions and reflections.

- **Sky and Fog**: Configure the sky and fog settings to match the atmosphere of your environment. Realistic sunsets, overcast skies, or dense fog can transform the mood.

Conclusion

Crafting natural environments in Blender is a rewarding creative endeavor. Whether you're building landscapes for games, animations, or architectural visualization, Blender's versatile tools empower you to create immersive and believable worlds. By paying attention to detail, studying real-world environments, and mastering Blender's modeling, texturing, and lighting features, you can breathe life into your digital landscapes and transport your audience to breathtaking natural settings.

17.2 Techniques for Large-Scale World Building

Creating large-scale worlds in Blender is a challenging but rewarding endeavor. Whether you're developing an open-world game, a massive architectural visualization project, or a detailed virtual environment, proper techniques are essential. In this section, we'll explore techniques and considerations for building expansive and intricate worlds within Blender.

Planning and Design

Large-scale world building starts with careful planning and design:

- **Concept and Story**: Define the concept and narrative of your world. What is its purpose? What story or experience do you want to convey to the audience?

- **Scale and Scope**: Determine the size and scope of your world. Consider the dimensions, boundaries, and key landmarks.

- **Layout and Organization**: Organize your world into logical zones or regions. Decide on the layout of cities, landscapes, and key points of interest.

- **Reference Material**: Gather reference materials, including maps, photographs, and concept art, to guide your design and maintain consistency.

Modular Assets and Procedural Generation

To efficiently build large worlds, use modular assets and procedural generation techniques:

- **Modular Assets**: Create reusable modular assets, such as building components, terrain pieces, and vegetation. This approach speeds up world assembly and ensures consistency.

- **Procedural Generation**: Leverage procedural generation tools in Blender to populate your world with elements like trees, rocks, or buildings. This reduces the manual workload and allows for dynamic variations.

```
# Procedural generation example in Blender

import bpy
```

```
# Create a procedural tree generator

bpy.ops.curve.tree_add(bevel=True, scale=2)

# Adjust parameters to generate different tree variations

tree_generator = bpy.context.object

tree_generator.levels = 3

tree_generator.seed = 12345
```

Level of Detail (LOD) Techniques

Maintaining performance in large-scale worlds is crucial. Implement Level of Detail (LOD) techniques to optimize the rendering of distant objects:

- **LOD Models**: Create simplified versions of objects for different levels of detail. Distant objects use low-poly versions to reduce the computational load.
- **Culling**: Implement occlusion culling and frustum culling techniques to avoid rendering objects that are not visible to the camera.
- **Texture Streaming**: Load high-resolution textures dynamically based on the camera's position to minimize memory usage.

Scene Management

Efficient scene management is essential for large worlds:

- **Collections**: Use collections in Blender to organize objects logically. Collections allow you to enable or disable groups of objects easily.

- **Scene Layers**: Utilize scene layers to divide your world into manageable sections. You can switch between layers to focus on specific areas during editing.

```
# Switching between scene layers

import bpy

# Activate a specific scene layer

bpy.context.view_layer.active_layer_collection = bpy.context.view_layer.layer_collection.children['Layer 1']
```

Collaboration and Version Control

When working on large-scale projects, collaboration and version control are critical:

- **Version Control Systems**: Use version control systems like Git to track changes, collaborate with team members, and maintain a history of your project.

- **Asset Management**: Implement an asset management system to keep track of models, textures, and other resources used in your world.

Conclusion

Building large-scale worlds in Blender is a complex and exciting undertaking. With careful planning, modular assets, procedural generation, LOD techniques, efficient scene management, and collaboration tools, you can bring expansive and immersive worlds to life. Whether you're creating games, architectural visualizations, or virtual environments, these techniques will help you manage the challenges of large-scale world building and deliver captivating experiences to your audience.

17.3 Integrating Ecology and Realism in Environmental Design

Creating realistic and ecologically sound environments in Blender adds depth and authenticity to your 3D projects. Whether you're designing a natural landscape, architectural visualization, or a virtual world, understanding ecology and realism is crucial. In this section, we'll explore techniques for integrating ecology and realism into your environmental design in Blender.

Ecological Considerations

Consider ecological factors when designing environments:

- **Biodiversity**: Mimic real-world ecosystems by including a variety of plant and animal species. Research the types of flora and fauna that thrive in the environment you're recreating.

- **Food Chains**: Model food chains and interactions between species. Predators and prey, herbivores and carnivores, and symbiotic relationships can add depth to your ecosystem.

- **Climate and Geography**: Base your environment on realistic climate and geographical features. Different climates support distinct ecosystems, so research how these factors influence your design.

- **Natural Processes**: Integrate natural processes like erosion, weathering, and plant growth into your environment. These processes give your world a sense of history and dynamism.

Realistic Flora and Fauna

To enhance realism, pay attention to the design and placement of plants and animals:

- **Botanical Accuracy**: Model plants with accurate botanical details. Pay attention to leaf shapes, textures, and growth patterns.

- **Behavioral Observation**: Observe real-world animals to understand their behaviors and movement patterns. Implement these observations when animating creatures in your environment.

- **Diversity**: Include a diverse range of plant and animal species. Incorporate variations in size, color, and behavior to mimic real ecosystems.

- **Habitat Variety**: Design various habitats within your environment, such as wetlands, forests, and grasslands. Each habitat supports unique species and vegetation.

Environmental Dynamics

Add realism by simulating environmental dynamics:

- **Weather Systems**: Incorporate weather patterns like rain, snow, and wind. These dynamic elements can affect the appearance and behavior of your environment.

- **Day-Night Cycle**: Implement a day-night cycle to simulate the passage of time. Different species may be active during the day or night.

```
# Creating a day-night cycle in Blender

import bpy

# Set the frame range for the day-night cycle

bpy.context.scene.frame_start = 1

bpy.context.scene.frame_end = 240

# Animate the sun's rotation to simulate the cycle

sun = bpy.data.objects['Sun']

sun.rotation_euler[2] = 0 # Start at sunrise

sun.keyframe_insert(data_path="rotation_euler", frame=1)

sun.rotation_euler[2] = 2 * 3.14159 # End at sunrise (360 degrees)

sun.keyframe_insert(data_path="rotation_euler", frame=240)
```

- **Seasonal Changes**: Introduce seasonal variations in your environment. Different seasons can affect vegetation, animal behavior, and the overall look of the environment.

Research and References

Incorporate research and references into your workflow:

- **Field Research**: If possible, conduct field research or visit real-world environments similar to your design. Observations and photographs can be invaluable references.

- **Scientific Literature**: Consult scientific literature and resources related to ecology, biology, and environmental science to ensure accuracy in your design.

- **Photographic References**: Use photographs of real-world environments and species as references. These references can guide your modeling and texturing.

Conclusion

Integrating ecology and realism into your environmental design in Blender elevates the quality and authenticity of your 3D projects. By considering ecological factors, modeling realistic flora and fauna, simulating environmental dynamics, and conducting thorough research, you can create environments that not only look visually stunning but also reflect the complexity and beauty of the natural world. Whether you're designing for entertainment, education, or artistic expression, these techniques will help you craft environments that resonate with your audience and convey a sense of ecological authenticity.

17.4 Utilizing Blender for Concept Art and Pre-Visualization

Blender is a powerful tool not only for creating final 3D scenes but also for concept art and pre-visualization. Concept artists and designers often use Blender to flesh out ideas, visualize concepts, and plan their projects before diving into full production. In this section, we'll explore how Blender can be a valuable asset for concept art and pre-visualization workflows.

Ideation and Sketching

Blender's 3D modeling and sculpting tools can be used for sketching and ideation:

- **Quick Mockups**: Create rough 3D mockups of environments, characters, or objects to visualize concepts. These don't need to be detailed but can help you explore ideas in 3D space.

- **Blockouts**: Use basic geometric shapes to block out scenes or architectural designs. This technique allows you to experiment with composition and layout.

- **Sculpting**: Blender's sculpting tools are excellent for shaping organic forms. Artists can quickly sketch creatures or characters to explore designs.

Rapid Prototyping

Blender enables rapid prototyping of assets and scenes:

- **Asset Creation**: Develop 3D assets like props, vehicles, or architectural elements to test how they fit into your project's world.

- **Scene Composition**: Experiment with different camera angles, lighting setups, and scene compositions to find the most visually engaging approach.

- **Lighting Tests**: Test various lighting scenarios and moods to see how they impact the overall atmosphere of your project.

```
# Setting up lighting in Blender
import bpy
# Add a point light
bpy.ops.object.light_add(type='POINT', location=(0, 0, 3))
# Configure light properties
light = bpy.context.object.data
light.energy = 1000.0 # Adjust the intensity
light.color = (1, 1, 1) # Set light color to white
```

Iterative Design

Blender allows for iterative design and refinement:

- **Layered Workflows**: Use Blender's layer system or collections to work in iterations. You can save different versions of your design within the same project file.
- **Version Control**: Implement version control practices to track changes and easily switch between different iterations of your project.

Storyboarding and Animatics

Blender is useful for creating storyboards and animatics:

- **Storyboarding**: Utilize the Grease Pencil tool to create storyboards directly in the 3D environment. This approach allows for easy adjustments and updates.

- **Animatics**: Create rough animatics to plan the timing and pacing of animated sequences. This helps visualize how scenes will play out.

```
# Grease Pencil example in Blender

import bpy

# Create a new grease pencil object

gpencil = bpy.data.grease_pencils.new('Storyboard')

# Switch to draw mode

bpy.context.view_layer.grease_pencil = gpencil

bpy.ops.gpencil.paint(mode='DRAW')
```

Export and Integration

Blender provides various export options for integrating your concept art and pre-visualization work into other software:

- **Image Renders**: Render still images or turntables of your 3D scenes for use in presentations, pitches, or further development.

- **Export to Other Software**: Export models, animations, or scenes to other software like Photoshop, After Effects, or game engines for further refinement or integration into larger projects.

Conclusion

Blender's versatility makes it an excellent tool for concept art and pre-visualization. Whether you're sketching out ideas, rapidly prototyping scenes, or creating storyboards and animatics, Blender's 3D capabilities empower artists and designers to visualize and iterate on their concepts efficiently. By incorporating Blender into your workflow, you can streamline the creative process, explore ideas in three dimensions, and ultimately bring your visions to life with greater clarity and precision.

17.5 Case Studies: Memorable Worlds Created in Blender

To appreciate the power and versatility of Blender in environmental design and world building, let's explore some case studies of memorable worlds and environments that have been brought to life using Blender's capabilities.

Case Study 1: "Sintel" - The Durian Open Movie Project

One of the most iconic Blender projects is "Sintel," a short film created by the Blender Institute. The film showcases Blender's capabilities in creating rich and detailed worlds, from mystical forests to ancient ruins. The project also highlights Blender's animation and character design capabilities.

The "Sintel" project demonstrates how Blender can be used for storytelling and world building, making it a valuable tool for animators and filmmakers. It showcased the software's ability to handle complex scenes, intricate character designs, and realistic environments.

Case Study 2: "Spring" - The Blender Animation Studio

"Spring" is another notable project from the Blender Animation Studio. This animated short film is known for its lush and vibrant natural environments. Blender was instrumental in creating the detailed forest settings, complete with realistic vegetation and lighting.

The project demonstrates Blender's capacity to generate immersive and visually striking natural environments. It also emphasizes the software's potential for crafting compelling narratives and storytelling within 3D worlds.

Case Study 3: Architectural Visualization Projects

Blender has gained popularity in architectural visualization, where designers and architects use it to bring building designs to life. Numerous architectural firms and visualization studios have successfully employed Blender to create realistic building interiors and exteriors, as well as detailed urban landscapes.

These projects showcase Blender's ability to create precise and visually stunning architectural environments. The software's modeling, rendering, and animation tools have made it a valuable asset in the field of architecture and urban planning.

Case Study 4: "Kaiju Fury!" - An Independent Game Project

"Kaiju Fury!" is an independent game project that leverages Blender for world building and character design. The game features massive monsters, detailed cityscapes, and dynamic environments, all created using Blender's 3D capabilities.

This project highlights Blender's suitability for game development, particularly in the creation of expansive game worlds and assets. It demonstrates the software's potential for indie game developers to bring their imaginative worlds to life on a budget.

Case Study 5: User-Created Environments

Blender's community of users continually produces stunning environments and worlds. Artists and 3D enthusiasts share their creations on various platforms, showcasing a wide range of environments, from fantastical landscapes to futuristic cityscapes.

These user-created environments illustrate the diverse applications of Blender in world building. They emphasize the software's role as a creative platform for individuals to express their artistic visions and share their virtual worlds with a global audience.

Conclusion

These case studies exemplify Blender's versatility and power in the realm of environmental design and world building. From film production and architectural visualization to independent game development and individual artistic expression, Blender has proven its effectiveness in creating memorable and immersive 3D worlds. As Blender continues to evolve and grow, it remains a valuable tool for professionals and enthusiasts alike, offering endless possibilities for crafting captivating and memorable virtual environments.

Chapter 18: Character Creation and Design

18.1 Fundamentals of Character Design in Blender

Character design is a fundamental aspect of 3D art, animation, and game development. Blender provides a comprehensive set of tools and features for creating, modeling, and animating characters. In this section, we'll explore the fundamentals of character design in Blender, covering key concepts and techniques.

Character Design Principles

Successful character design begins with understanding the following principles:

- **Silhouette**: A character's silhouette should be distinctive and instantly recognizable. It helps viewers identify the character at a glance.

- **Proportion**: Maintain consistent proportions for your character's body parts. While stylization is encouraged, maintaining proportion within your chosen style is crucial.

- **Appeal**: A well-designed character should be visually appealing. Consider the character's personality and role in your project when designing its appearance.

- **Functionality**: Think about the character's role and functionality within your project. Their design should align with their purpose and story.

Character Concept and Reference

Before you start modeling, create a character concept and gather references:

- **Concept Art**: Develop concept art or sketches to visualize your character. This serves as a reference for modeling.

- **Reference Images**: Collect reference images that align with your character's design and style. These images can help you achieve realism or adhere to a specific art direction.

Character Modeling

Blender offers various methods for character modeling:

- **Box Modeling**: Start with basic shapes like cubes and cylinders and gradually refine the model. Box modeling is versatile and suitable for a wide range of character types.

- **Sculpting**: Use Blender's sculpting tools to create organic and detailed character models. Sculpting is ideal for creatures, monsters, and characters with complex forms.

- **Retopology**: After sculpting, perform retopology to create a clean and optimized mesh suitable for animation. This step ensures proper deformation during rigging and animation.

Rigging and Animation

Character design goes hand in hand with rigging and animation:

- **Armatures**: Use armatures to create a skeletal structure for your character. Armatures define how the character's mesh deforms during animation.

- **Rigging**: Assign bones to specific parts of your character, such as limbs, joints, and facial features. Rigging controls the character's movement and expressions.

```
# Creating a basic armature in Blender

import bpy

# Add an armature object

bpy.ops.object.armature_add()

# Enter Edit Mode to manipulate bones

bpy.ops.object.mode_set(mode='EDIT')
```

- **Animation**: Animate your character by setting keyframes for bone movements and facial expressions. Blender's animation tools allow for precise control over character motion.

Texturing and Shading

Texture your character for added realism and detail:

- **UV Mapping**: Unwrap your character's mesh and create UV maps to apply textures accurately.

- **Material Nodes**: Use Blender's material nodes to create complex and realistic shaders for your character's skin, clothing, and accessories.

- **Texture Painting**: Paint textures directly onto your character's model using Blender's texture painting tools.

Character Expression

Character design isn't complete without facial expressions:

- **Shape Keys**: Create shape keys (blend shapes) to control facial expressions. Each shape key represents a different facial pose, allowing for a range of emotions.

- **Drivers**: Use drivers to automate facial expressions based on bone movement or control sliders.

Conclusion

Character design is a multifaceted process that involves creativity, technical skills, and attention to detail. Blender's robust set of modeling, rigging, and animation tools empowers artists and designers to bring their characters to life. By adhering to design principles, concept development, and proper modeling techniques, you can create compelling and memorable characters that enhance your 3D projects, animations, or games.

18.2 From Concept to Model: The Character Creation Process

The process of character creation in Blender involves several stages, from conceptualizing your character to bringing them to life as a 3D model. In this section, we'll dive into the detailed steps of character creation, highlighting the workflow and techniques commonly used by artists and 3D modelers.

Conceptualization and Design

Character creation starts with a clear concept and design:

- **Character Profile**: Define your character's backstory, personality, and role within your project. This information informs their appearance and behavior.

- **Concept Art**: Create concept art or sketches to visualize your character. Consider aspects like costume, hairstyle, and unique features.

- **Reference Gathering**: Collect reference images that align with your character's design and style. These references serve as visual guidelines during modeling.

Model Blocking and Proportions

Once you have a concept, begin blocking out the character's basic shape:

- **Box Modeling**: Start with basic shapes like cubes and cylinders to create a rough 3D silhouette of your character. This step establishes the character's proportions and overall form.

- **Proportional Accuracy**: Ensure that the character's body parts are in proportion to each other. Maintain consistency while considering the style and design of your character.

Detailed Modeling

After blocking out the character's form, proceed with detailed modeling:

- **Sculpting**: Use Blender's sculpting tools for organic and detailed modeling. Sculpting allows you to add finer details to the character's body and features.

- **Retopology**: Perform retopology to create a clean and optimized mesh. The retopologized mesh is better suited for rigging and animation.

- **Facial Features**: Pay special attention to facial features. Model the character's eyes, nose, mouth, and ears with precision, as these are crucial for conveying expressions.

```
# Entering sculpt mode in Blender

import bpy

# Select the character model

character = bpy.data.objects['Character']

# Enter Sculpt Mode

bpy.context.view_layer.objects.active = character

bpy.ops.sculpt.sculptmode_toggle()
```

Rigging and Armature

Rigging is essential for character animation:

- **Armature Creation**: Build an armature (skeletal structure) for your character. The armature defines how the character's mesh deforms during animation.

- **Bone Rigging**: Assign bones to specific parts of your character, such as limbs, joints, and facial features. Rigging controls the character's movement and expressions.

- **Weight Painting**: Use weight painting to assign influence to bones. This determines how much each bone affects the deformation of the character's mesh.

```
# Adding an armature to the character in Blender

import bpy

# Select the character mesh

character = bpy.data.objects['Character']

# Add an armature object

bpy.ops.object.armature_add()

# Parent the character mesh to the armature with automatic weights

bpy.context.view_layer.objects.active = character

bpy.ops.object.parent_set(type='ARMATURE_AUTO')
```

UV Mapping and Texturing

Texturing adds realism and detail to your character:

- **UV Unwrapping**: Unwrap your character's mesh to create UV maps. UV maps allow you to apply textures accurately.

- **Texture Painting**: Use Blender's texture painting tools to paint textures directly onto your character's model. This step includes detailing skin, clothing, and accessories.

- **Material Shading**: Create shaders using Blender's material nodes to achieve realistic skin, hair, and clothing materials.

Facial Rigging and Animation

To bring your character to life, focus on facial rigging and animation:

- **Shape Keys**: Create shape keys (blend shapes) to control facial expressions. Each shape key represents a different facial pose, allowing for a range of emotions.

- **Drivers**: Use drivers to automate facial expressions based on bone movement or control sliders. This simplifies the animation process and adds expressiveness to your character.

Conclusion

The character creation process in Blender is a comprehensive and creative endeavor. By following these steps, from conceptualization to modeling, rigging, and animation, you can transform your character concept into a fully realized 3D model ready for use in animations, games, or other 3D projects. Blender's versatile tools and features provide artists and 3D modelers with the flexibility to bring a wide range of characters to life, each with its unique personality and design.

18.3 Techniques for Realistic Human Characters

Creating realistic human characters is a common and challenging task in 3D character design, especially in Blender. Realism involves achieving accurate proportions, lifelike skin textures, and believable facial expressions. In this section, we'll explore techniques and tips for creating realistic human characters in Blender.

Reference and Anatomy

Start by studying human anatomy and gathering references:

- **Anatomy Study**: Familiarize yourself with human anatomy, including muscle structure, bone placement, and facial features. Understanding anatomy is essential for achieving realism.

- **Reference Photos**: Collect high-quality reference photos of real people who resemble your character's intended appearance. These photos serve as visual guides during modeling and texturing.

High-Quality Modeling

Realistic modeling is key to creating convincing human characters:

- **Proportional Accuracy**: Ensure that the character's body proportions are accurate. Use reference images and anatomical knowledge to guide your modeling.

- **Facial Details**: Pay close attention to facial details, including the eyes, nose, mouth, and ears. Model these features with precision to capture subtle nuances.

- **Topology**: Maintain clean and optimized topology. Proper edge flow is crucial for smooth deformations during rigging and animation.

Texturing and Shading

Achieving realistic skin is a critical aspect of human character design:

- **Skin Textures**: Use high-resolution skin textures to add fine details such as pores, wrinkles, and freckles. Subsurface scattering (SSS) shaders can enhance the skin's translucency.

- **Displacement Maps**: Apply displacement maps to add depth to the skin's surface. This technique creates realistic skin bumps and imperfections.

- **Microdetails**: Don't overlook microdetails like skin pores and fine hairs. These subtle elements contribute to the character's realism.

```
# Applying a displacement map in Blender

import bpy

# Select the character's mesh

character = bpy.data.objects['Character']

# Add a displacement modifier

mod = character.modifiers.new(name="Displacement", type='DISPLACE')

# Load the displacement map image

texture = bpy.data.images.load('path_to_displacement_map.png')

# Set the displacement map as the modifier's texture

mod.texture = texture
```

Hair and Grooming

Realistic hair and grooming are essential for human characters:

- **Hair Particles**: Use Blender's hair particles system to create hair and facial hair. Adjust settings like density, length, and curl to achieve the desired look.

- **Grooming**: Groom the hair by combing, shaping, and styling it to match the character's appearance. The grooming process can be time-consuming but adds realism.

Rigging and Facial Expression

Realistic rigging and facial expressions are crucial for bringing your character to life:

- **Facial Rigging**: Create a comprehensive facial rig with bone controls for various facial muscles. This allows for a wide range of expressions.

- **Blend Shapes**: Implement blend shapes (shape keys) to control facial expressions more intuitively. Each blend shape represents a different expression, making animation easier.

Lighting and Rendering

Proper lighting and rendering contribute to realism:

- **Three-Point Lighting**: Use a three-point lighting setup to illuminate your character. This setup consists of key, fill, and rim lights to create depth and highlights.

- **HDRI Lighting**: Employ high dynamic range images (HDRI) for realistic lighting and reflections. HDRI maps capture real-world lighting conditions.

Post-Processing

Post-processing can enhance the final result:

- **Color Grading**: Apply color grading techniques to adjust the character's overall color palette and mood.

- **Depth of Field**: Add depth of field effects to focus on specific parts of the character while blurring the background, simulating a camera lens.

Iteration and Feedback

Character design often involves iteration and feedback:

- **Feedback Loop**: Seek feedback from peers or mentors to identify areas for improvement. Iteratively refine your character based on critiques.

- **Experimentation**: Don't be afraid to experiment with different techniques and styles. Each project can be a learning experience.

Creating realistic human characters in Blender is a rewarding endeavor that requires a combination of artistic skill, technical knowledge, and attention to detail. By following these techniques and continually refining your skills, you can create characters that appear lifelike and engage viewers in your 3D projects.

18.4 Stylized Characters: Creating Unique

Personalities

Stylized character design is a popular and versatile approach in 3D art, animation, and game development. Unlike realistic characters, stylized characters emphasize exaggeration, simplicity, and uniqueness. In this section, we'll explore techniques for creating stylized characters in Blender and how to infuse them with unique personalities.

Concept and Style

Stylized character design begins with a clear concept and artistic style:

- **Character Concept**: Define your character's personality, backstory, and role within your project. Consider what makes them unique and memorable.

- **Artistic Style**: Determine the artistic style you want to achieve. Stylization can range from cartoony and exaggerated to minimalist and abstract.

- **Reference Art**: Gather reference images and artwork that align with your chosen style. These references serve as visual inspiration during the design process.

Unique Silhouette and Proportions

Stylized characters often have distinctive silhouettes and proportions:

- **Silhouette Design**: Focus on creating a silhouette that stands out and is easily recognizable. Unique shapes and exaggerated features can contribute to a memorable silhouette.

- **Proportional Play**: Embrace creative freedom with proportions. Stylized characters may have oversized heads, exaggerated limbs, or unconventional body shapes to emphasize their personality.

Simple Geometry

Simplicity is key in stylized character design:

- **Geometry Reduction**: Keep the character's geometry relatively simple. Avoid unnecessary details and intricacies that might be present in realistic characters.

- **Clean Lines**: Use clean and well-defined lines to highlight the character's features and contours. Bold outlines can enhance the stylization.

Expressive Faces and Eyes

Stylized characters often have expressive faces:

- **Cartoony Expressions**: Embrace exaggerated facial expressions to convey emotions and personality. Cartoony eyes, mouths, and brows can be highly expressive.

- **Large Eyes**: Enlarged and expressive eyes are a common feature in many stylized characters. They can convey a wide range of emotions.

Texturing and Color

Texturing plays a vital role in stylized character design:

- **Flat Colors**: Consider using flat, non-photorealistic colors rather than complex textures. Solid colors or cell-shaded styles can contribute to the character's stylized appearance.

- **Painted Textures**: Use hand-painted textures for a painterly effect. This approach allows for more artistic control over the character's appearance.

Hair and Accessories

Stylized characters often have unique hairstyles and accessories:

- **Exaggerated Hair**: Create exaggerated and stylized hair designs that complement the character's overall style.

- **Accessories**: Incorporate distinctive accessories, such as hats, glasses, or jewelry, to enhance the character's personality.

Rigging and Animation

Stylized characters can have lively and exaggerated animations:

- **Cartoony Movements**: Animate your character with cartoony and exaggerated movements that align with their personality. Think about how their unique traits influence their actions.

- **Facial Expressions**: Prioritize expressive facial animations that amplify the character's emotions and quirks.

Lighting and Rendering

Stylized characters can benefit from unique lighting setups:

- **Toon Shading**: Consider using toon or cel shading techniques for rendering. These techniques emphasize the character's contours and edges.

- **Stylized Lighting**: Experiment with unconventional and stylized lighting setups that enhance the character's appearance and mood.

Iteration and Creativity

Creating stylized characters is an opportunity for creativity and experimentation:

- **Iterate and Refine**: Don't hesitate to iterate on your character design. Experiment with different styles and features until you achieve the desired look.

- **Unique Personalities**: Infuse your character with a unique personality that reflects their style and design. Consider their backstory and traits when animating them.

Stylized character design in Blender offers artists and creators the freedom to explore unique and imaginative characters. By focusing on simplicity, exaggeration, and expressive features, you can craft stylized characters that leave a lasting impression and contribute to the distinctiveness of your 3D projects, animations, or games.

18.5 Rigging and Animating Characters for Film and Games

Rigging and animation are essential aspects of character design in Blender, whether you're creating characters for films, games, or other interactive media. In this section, we'll delve into the processes of rigging and animating characters, focusing on techniques that are particularly useful for character animation in both film and game development.

Character Rigging

Character rigging involves creating a skeletal structure and controls for your character:

- **Armature Setup**: Start by adding an armature to your character. The armature defines the character's bone structure and how it deforms during animation.

- **Bone Placement**: Carefully position bones to match the character's anatomy. Rigging typically includes bones for limbs, spine, facial features, and more.

- **Inverse Kinematics (IK)**: Implement IK constraints for limbs like arms and legs to simplify animation. IK allows you to control the end of a chain of bones while the rest follow.

```
# Creating an IK constraint in Blender

import bpy

# Select the armature object

armature = bpy.data.objects['Armature']
```

```
# Select the bone you want to apply IK to

bone = armature.pose.bones['IK_Bone']

# Add an IK constraint

ik_constraint = bone.constraints.new(type='IK')

ik_constraint.target = bpy.data.objects['IK_Target']
```

Weight Painting

Weight painting determines how bones influence the character's mesh during animation:

- **Weight Assignments**: Use weight painting to assign vertex groups to bones. This controls how much each bone affects the deformation of the character's mesh.

- **Smooth Transitions**: Ensure smooth transitions between bone influences by carefully painting weights. Avoid harsh seams or unnatural deformations.

Facial Rigging and Blend Shapes

Facial rigging is crucial for character expressions:

- **Bone-Based Facial Rig**: Create a bone-based facial rig to control facial expressions. Each bone corresponds to a facial muscle or feature.

- **Blend Shapes (Shape Keys)**: Implement blend shapes or shape keys for more intuitive facial animation. Blend shapes allow you to control various expressions with sliders.

Animation Principles

Animating characters effectively requires an understanding of animation principles:

- **Keyframes**: Set keyframes to define the character's pose and movements at specific frames. Keyframes are the foundation of animation in Blender.

- **Easing**: Apply easing to achieve realistic and smooth animations. Easing involves gradually slowing down or accelerating the character's movement.

- **Timing**: Pay attention to timing and spacing in your animations. Timing determines how quickly or slowly actions occur, while spacing affects the distribution of keyframes.

Character Animation in Games

In game development, character animation involves additional considerations:

- **Character Controllers**: Implement character controllers or input systems to enable player control. These systems translate player input into character movements.

- **Animation Blending**: Use animation blending to smoothly transition between different character animations. This allows for fluid movement and interactions in games.

- **Physics and Collisions**: Consider physics and collision detection to ensure that characters interact realistically with the game environment.

 # Implementing character movement in a game engine (e.g., Unity or Unreal)

 # Example Unity C# code for character movement

```
using UnityEngine;

public class CharacterController : MonoBehaviour

{

public float speed = 5.0f;

void Update()

{

float horizontalInput = Input.GetAxis("Horizontal");

float verticalInput = Input.GetAxis("Vertical");

Vector3 moveDirection = new Vector3(horizontalInput, 0, verticalInput);

moveDirection.Normalize();

transform.Translate(moveDirection * speed * Time.deltaTime);

}

}
```

Lip Syncing and Facial Expressions

For character dialogue and emotion expression, consider lip syncing and facial expressions:

- **Lip Syncing**: Sync character lip movements with audio using phoneme-based animation or automated lip-syncing tools.
- **Facial Expression Animation**: Animate facial expressions to match the character's emotions and dialogue. Blend shapes or bone-based rigs can be used for this purpose.

Character rigging and animation are complex but rewarding processes in Blender. Whether you're creating characters for cinematic storytelling or interactive games, a well-rigged and animated character can captivate audiences and enhance the overall quality of your project. Understanding the principles of rigging and animation, as well as considering the specific needs of your medium, will help you bring your characters to life effectively.

19.1 The Basics of Compositing in Blender

Compositing is an integral part of the 3D rendering pipeline that allows you to combine and manipulate multiple images or image layers to create a final, polished render. In Blender, compositing is done using the Compositor, a node-based system that offers a wide range of tools and possibilities. In this section, we'll explore the basics of compositing in Blender, including how to set up the Compositor, work with nodes, and perform common compositing tasks.

Accessing the Compositor

To access the Compositor in Blender, follow these steps:

1. Open Blender and load your 3D scene.
2. Switch to the "Compositing" workspace by selecting it from the top menu bar or changing the workspace type in the workspace dropdown menu.
3. In the Compositing workspace, you'll find two main areas: the Node Editor and the Viewer Node. The Node Editor is where you'll build your compositing node network, and the Viewer Node displays the final composited result.

Node-Based Compositing

Blender's Compositor uses a node-based approach, where you connect various nodes to create a network that defines the compositing process. Here are some essential nodes and their functions:

- **Image Node**: Input your render or image sequences as image nodes. These nodes serve as the starting point for your compositing.

- **Color Nodes**: Nodes like "Color Balance," "Hue/Saturation," and "Brightness/Contrast" allow you to adjust the color and tone of your images.

- **Alpha Over Node**: Use this node to overlay one image or sequence over another, taking into account alpha (transparency) information.

- **Blur and Sharpen Nodes**: Apply blurs or sharpening effects to images using nodes like "Blur" and "Filter."

- **Composite Node**: The final result of your compositing network is often connected to a "Composite" node, which outputs the fully composited image.

Basic Compositing Tasks

Let's look at some common compositing tasks and how to achieve them in Blender:

1. Color Correction

To perform color correction on your rendered image, you can use nodes like "Color Balance" and "Hue/Saturation." Connect these nodes to your image input and adjust their settings to achieve the desired color correction.

2. Adding Glows and Effects

For adding glows and other effects to specific parts of your image, you can use nodes like "Glare" and "Lens Distortion." These nodes create various visual effects, and you can control their intensity and parameters.

3. Background Replacement

If you want to replace the background of your rendered image with a different image or footage, use the "Alpha Over" node. Connect your foreground image (rendered scene) to one input and the background image to the other. The alpha channel will ensure proper blending.

4. Depth of Field

To apply a depth of field effect to your rendered image, you can use the "Defocus" node. Connect your image to the input, and the node will simulate the blurring effect based on depth information.

5. Render Layers and Passes

Blender allows you to render different elements of your scene as separate render layers and passes. You can then composite these elements individually and combine them in the Compositor to have more control over the final result.

Node Organization and Workflow

As your compositing node network becomes more complex, it's essential to keep it organized. You can use frames and labels to group related nodes and add comments to nodes for clarity.

When working in the Compositor, it's a good practice to render the result to a new image or image sequence format (e.g., PNG or OpenEXR) using the "File Output" node. This ensures that your composited image is saved separately from your original render.

Blender's Compositor is a powerful tool that allows you to enhance the quality of your 3D renders and create stunning visual effects. By understanding the basics of node-based compositing, you can take full advantage of this feature to achieve your desired results in Blender.

19.2 Techniques for Effective Color Grading

Color grading is a fundamental aspect of compositing in Blender that allows you to enhance the visual aesthetics of your rendered images or animations. It involves adjusting the colors, contrast, and overall look of your composition to achieve a desired mood or style. In this section, we'll explore techniques for effective color grading in Blender's Compositor.

Color Grading Nodes

Blender offers several nodes specifically designed for color grading. These nodes include:

- **Color Balance Node**: The Color Balance node allows you to adjust the shadows, midtones, and highlights of your image separately. You can control the color balance and brightness of each range to achieve the desired look.

- **Color Correction Node**: The Color Correction node provides various adjustments, such as contrast, saturation, brightness, and gamma correction. It's a versatile tool for overall color adjustments.

- **Hue/Saturation Node**: This node lets you manipulate the hue, saturation, and lightness of specific colors in your composition. It's handy for making selective color changes.

- **RGB Curves Node**: The RGB Curves node gives you precise control over the tonal range and color channels of your image. You can create custom curves to fine-tune the color and contrast.

Workflow for Color Grading

Effective color grading often involves a structured workflow. Here's a step-by-step process for color grading in Blender:

1. **Load Your Image**: Start by adding your rendered image or image sequence to the Compositor as an image node. This serves as your base for color grading.
2. **Organize Your Node Tree**: Keep your node tree organized by using frames, labels, and comments. Group related color grading nodes together for clarity.
3. **Adjust Exposure**: Begin with basic exposure adjustments using the Color Correction node. You can control the overall brightness and contrast of your image at this stage.
4. **Correct Color Balance**: Use the Color Balance node to fine-tune the color balance in your image. Adjust shadows, midtones, and highlights to achieve the desired color temperature.
5. **Enhance Contrast**: If needed, apply contrast adjustments using the RGB Curves node. You can create an S-curve to increase overall contrast while preserving details.
6. **Selective Color Adjustments**: If specific colors need adjustment, employ the Hue/Saturation node. For example, you can desaturate or boost the saturation of specific hues.
7. **Creative Grading**: At this stage, you can get creative with your color grading. Experiment with different nodes and adjustments to achieve the desired mood or style for your composition.
8. **View Node**: Connect a Viewer node to preview your color-graded image. This node displays the final composited result in the Viewer Node area.
9. **Render or Save**: Once you're satisfied with the color grading, render the result to a new image or image sequence format. You can use the "File Output" node to save the graded image.

Color Grading Tips

Here are some additional tips for effective color grading in Blender:

- **Reference Images**: Use reference images or color grading references from movies, photographs, or artwork to guide your grading decisions and achieve a specific look.

- **Consistency**: Maintain consistency in your color grading throughout a project to ensure that all scenes or shots have a cohesive visual style.

- **Subtle Adjustments**: Sometimes, less is more. Small, subtle adjustments can have a significant impact on the overall look without overdoing it.

- **Backup and Versioning**: Save different versions of your color grading node tree or create backups before making significant changes. This allows you to experiment without losing your progress.

- **Feedback**: Seek feedback from peers or colleagues to get a fresh perspective on your color grading choices.

Color grading is a creative and essential step in the compositing process that can transform the mood and visual appeal of your rendered scenes. By mastering the color grading nodes in Blender's Compositor and following a structured workflow, you can achieve stunning and professional-looking results in your 3D projects.

19.3 Integrating 3D Elements into Live Footage

Integrating 3D elements into live footage, often referred to as "matchmoving" or "camera tracking," is a crucial skill in visual effects and compositing. Blender provides powerful tools for seamlessly combining 3D objects or animations with real-world footage, allowing you to create stunning and realistic visual effects. In this section, we'll explore the process of integrating 3D elements into live footage using Blender.

The Matchmoving Process

The matchmoving process involves several key steps:

1. **Film Your Footage**: Start by capturing the live footage you want to integrate with 3D elements. Ensure that you have enough tracking markers or features in the scene for accurate tracking.
2. **Import Footage**: In Blender, import your live footage as an image sequence or video file. You can do this by adding an "Image" node in the Compositor and selecting your footage.
3. **Tracking**: Blender's motion tracking feature allows you to track the movement of objects or the camera in the live footage. To track, go to the "Movie Clip Editor" workspace, load your footage, and add tracking markers to objects or features that have distinct motion.

```
# Example Python code for tracking in Blender

import bpy

# Switch to the Motion Tracking workspace
```

```
bpy.context.window.workspace =
bpy.data.workspaces['Motion Tracking']

# Load the live footage

clip = bpy.data.movieclips.load('/path/to/your/
footage.mp4')

# Create a new tracking scene

scene = bpy.context.scene

motion_track = scene.motion_track_add()

motion_track.name = "MyTrackingScene"

# Set the clip for the tracking scene

motion_track.clip = clip

# Add tracking markers and track them

# ...
```

1. **Solving the Camera**: After tracking markers, solve the camera motion to determine the camera's position and orientation for each frame. Blender's "Solve Camera Motion" button automates this process.
2. **Scene Setup**: Create or import the 3D elements you want to integrate into the live footage. Ensure that the camera in your 3D scene matches the tracked camera's movement.
3. **Scene Integration**: Place the 3D elements into your 3D scene, matching their position and orientation to the live footage. Use constraints or parenting to ensure they follow the tracked camera correctly.
4. **Render 3D Elements**: Render the 3D elements with a

transparent background so that they can be composited onto the live footage.

5. **Compositing**: In the Compositor, combine the live footage and 3D elements. Use the "Alpha Over" node to overlay the 3D elements onto the live footage, considering lighting and shadows.
6. **Fine-Tuning**: Fine-tune the integration by adjusting color grading, lighting, and shadows to ensure that the 3D elements blend seamlessly with the live footage.

Tips for Successful Integration

Here are some tips for achieving successful integration of 3D elements into live footage:

- **Tracking Markers**: Place tracking markers or features in the live footage that have distinct and trackable motion. High-contrast markers are often used.

- **Camera Lens Data**: Ensure that you input accurate camera lens data (e.g., focal length, sensor size) when solving the camera motion. This information is critical for a precise match.

- **Match Lighting**: Pay close attention to the lighting conditions in both the live footage and the 3D scene. Match the lighting direction, intensity, and color to create a convincing blend.

- **Shadows and Reflections**: Add shadows and reflections to the 3D elements to make them appear more realistic in the live environment.

- **Depth of Field**: If the live footage has a shallow depth of field, apply the same depth of field effect to the 3D elements to maintain realism.

- **Render Passes**: Render separate passes for the 3D elements, such as shadows, reflections, and ambient occlusion, and composite them individually for more control.

Integrating 3D elements into live footage is a complex but rewarding process that opens up a world of possibilities for visual effects and compositing. Blender's robust motion tracking and compositing tools make it a powerful choice for this task, allowing you to create impressive and realistic scenes that seamlessly blend the virtual and real worlds.

19.4 Achieving Cinematic Looks in Blender

Creating a cinematic look in your Blender compositing projects involves enhancing the visual quality and atmosphere of your scenes to mimic the aesthetics of a cinematic film. Whether you're working on animations, still images, or videos, achieving a cinematic look can significantly elevate the overall impact of your work. In this section, we'll explore various techniques and tools in Blender for achieving cinematic looks.

1. Aspect Ratio and Composition

Cinematic productions often use specific aspect ratios to frame their shots. In Blender, you can adjust the aspect ratio in the Output properties of the Render tab. Common cinematic ratios include 2.39:1 (widescreen) and 1.85:1. Additionally, pay attention to composition techniques like the rule of thirds, leading lines, and framing to create visually appealing shots.

2. Color Grading

Color grading plays a crucial role in achieving a cinematic look. Use nodes like Color Balance, Hue/Saturation, and RGB Curves to fine-tune the colors, contrast, and mood of your scenes. Experiment with warm or cool color palettes to evoke different emotions. The use of color grading can transform a bland render into a cinematic masterpiece.

```
# Example color grading node setup in Blender

import bpy

# Access the Compositor

compositor = bpy.context.scene.node_tree

# Add a Color Balance node

color_balance = compositor.nodes.new(type='CompositorNodeColorBalance')

# Adjust settings for shadows, midtones, and highlights

color_balance.shadows = (0.9, 1.0, 1.0)

color_balance.midtones = (1.0, 0.9, 0.8)

color_balance.highlights = (1.0, 1.0, 1.0)
```

3. Depth of Field

Depth of field (DOF) adds a cinematic touch by focusing on a specific subject while blurring the background or foreground. In

Blender, you can enable DOF in the Camera settings. Adjust the focus distance and f-stop to control the depth of field effect. This technique draws the viewer's attention to key elements in your scene.

4. Motion Blur

Motion blur simulates the way objects appear blurred when in motion, creating a sense of realism. You can enable motion blur in the Render settings under the Motion Blur section. Adjust the shutter speed and samples to control the intensity of the motion blur effect.

5. Filmic Color Management

Blender's Filmic color management transforms the way colors are processed, making it easier to achieve a cinematic look. In the Color Management tab of the Render properties, select the Filmic option from the Look dropdown menu. This provides you with a wider dynamic range and more control over the tonal response.

6. Film Grain and Vignetting

Adding a subtle amount of film grain and vignetting can contribute to the cinematic atmosphere. Blender's Compositor offers a node called "Noise" that you can use to introduce controlled film grain. For vignetting, use the "Lens Distortion" node, adjusting the settings to create a gentle darkening effect at the edges of the frame.

7. Lighting and Shadows

Pay meticulous attention to lighting and shadows. Use soft lighting techniques like three-point lighting to create depth and dimension in your scenes. Experiment with volumetric lighting and shadow quality settings to achieve the desired cinematic ambience. Accurate lighting and shadows can make a significant difference in the final look.

8. Post-Processing Effects

Consider adding post-processing effects like bloom, glare, and lens flares to enhance the visual appeal of your scenes. You can achieve these effects using nodes in the Compositor. These effects simulate camera imperfections and add a layer of cinematic style.

Achieving a cinematic look in Blender is a creative process that involves careful attention to details, color, lighting, and composition. By applying these techniques and experimenting with different settings, you can transform your Blender projects into cinematic masterpieces that captivate and immerse your audience.

19.5 Case Studies: Successful Compositing Projects

To gain a deeper understanding of compositing in Blender and its real-world applications, let's explore some case studies of successful compositing projects that showcase the versatility and power of Blender's compositing capabilities.

1. Starship Attack (Sci-Fi Short Film)

Project Overview: In this sci-fi short film, Blender was used to composite CGI starships into live-action footage. The goal was to create epic space battles and seamless integration of the starships with the actors and practical effects.

Compositing Techniques:

- Motion tracking was used to match the camera movement of the live-action footage.

- Extensive color grading and lens effects were applied to achieve a cinematic look.

- Realistic lighting and shadows were added to the CGI starships to match the on-set lighting.

- Motion blur and depth of field were used to enhance the realism of the starships' movement.

2. Fantasy Forest (Animated Short Film)

Project Overview: In this animated short film, Blender's compositing capabilities were used to composite 3D characters and creatures into a vibrant and magical forest environment.

Compositing Techniques:

- The forest environment was created using Blender's 3D modeling and texturing tools.

- Motion tracking was employed to integrate animated characters seamlessly into the forest scenes.

- Depth-based compositing techniques were used to simulate fog and depth of field.

- Color grading and post-processing effects were applied to achieve a dreamy and enchanting atmosphere.

3. Historical Reconstruction (Documentary)

Project Overview: In a historical documentary, Blender was used for compositing to recreate historical events and locations. The goal was to provide viewers with a realistic visual representation of historical settings.

Compositing Techniques:

- Blender's camera tracking feature was utilized to match the camera movement in archival footage.
- Accurate 3D models of historical buildings and landmarks were created and composited into live-action footage.
- Realistic lighting and shading were crucial for achieving historical accuracy.
- Extensive color grading was applied to match the visual style of the documentary.

4. Product Visualization (Commercial)

Project Overview: In a commercial project, Blender's compositing capabilities were employed to showcase a product in a visually appealing and dynamic way.

Compositing Techniques:

- 3D product models were created and composited into live-action scenes.
- Motion tracking was used to ensure the product appeared integrated into various environments.

- Attention to lighting and reflections on the product was crucial for realism.

- Post-processing effects such as glows and lens flares were added to highlight the product's features.

5. Architectural Visualization (Real Estate)

Project Overview: In the field of real estate, Blender was used for architectural visualization and compositing. The goal was to present architectural designs in a compelling and realistic manner.

Compositing Techniques:

- 3D models of buildings and interiors were created and integrated into live-action drone footage.

- Motion tracking ensured the 3D models appeared stable and realistic within the footage.

- Lighting and shadows were meticulously adjusted to match the real-world lighting conditions.

- Post-processing techniques, including color correction and lens effects, enhanced the visual appeal of the architectural visualization.

These case studies illustrate the diverse applications of Blender's compositing capabilities in various industries, from filmmaking and animation to architecture and product visualization. They highlight the importance of motion tracking, realistic lighting, color grading, and post-processing effects in achieving successful compositing results. Blender's versatility and robust feature set make it a valuable tool for artists and professionals across different fields.

20.1 Emerging Trends in 3D Graphics and Blender

The field of 3D graphics and computer-generated imagery (CGI) is constantly evolving, driven by technological advancements and creative innovations. Blender, as an open-source and community-driven software, remains at the forefront of these developments. In this section, we'll explore some emerging trends in 3D graphics and how Blender is adapting to and contributing to these changes.

1. Real-Time Rendering

One of the most significant trends in 3D graphics is the shift towards real-time rendering. With the growing demand for interactive experiences in gaming, architecture, and virtual reality, real-time rendering engines like Eevee have gained prominence. Blender's Eevee renderer offers real-time feedback and has become a valuable tool for artists and designers who require quick previews of their work.

2. AI and Machine Learning

Artificial intelligence (AI) and machine learning have made significant inroads in 3D graphics. These technologies are used for tasks such as character animation, procedural content generation, and denoising. Blender is exploring ways to integrate AI-driven tools to streamline workflows and enhance the creative process.

3. Virtual Production

Virtual production techniques, popularized by the film industry, involve the integration of real-time CGI with live-action footage. Blender's real-time capabilities make it a suitable choice for virtual production, allowing filmmakers to visualize and manipulate CGI elements on set, enhancing the overall creative process.

4. Augmented Reality (AR) and Mixed Reality (MR)

AR and MR applications are becoming more prevalent, spanning industries from gaming to education and training. Blender's flexibility makes it a valuable tool for creating 3D assets and content for AR and MR experiences. The ability to export models and animations to AR and MR platforms is a growing requirement.

```
# Example Python code for exporting Blender models to AR/VR formats

import bpy

# Select the objects to export

bpy.ops.object.select_all(action='DESELECT')

bpy.context.view_layer.objects.active = None

bpy.data.objects['MyModel'].select_set(True)

# Export to AR/VR format (e.g., FBX)

bpy.ops.export_scene.fbx(filepath='/path/to/exported/model.fbx', use_selection=True)
```

5. Generative Adversarial Networks (GANs)

GANs are being used to generate realistic textures, environments, and characters. Blender's support for procedural texturing and node-based workflows aligns well with GAN-driven content generation. Artists can leverage GAN-generated content to accelerate their creative processes.

6. Open-Source Collaboration

Blender's open-source philosophy continues to foster collaboration within the 3D graphics community. The Blender Foundation actively seeks partnerships and collaborations with other software developers, studios, and artists to push the boundaries of what's possible in 3D graphics.

7. Educational Initiatives

Blender's user-friendly interface and accessibility make it an ideal tool for educational purposes. Emerging trends include the integration of Blender into educational curricula and the creation of online tutorials and courses. Blender's community-driven approach encourages knowledge sharing and learning.

As Blender evolves, it remains a versatile and forward-looking tool in the ever-changing landscape of 3D graphics. Whether it's real-time rendering, AI integration, or emerging AR and VR applications, Blender's commitment to open-source principles and collaboration ensures that it continues to be a platform of choice for artists, developers, and educators shaping the future of 3D graphics.

20.2 The Role of AI and Machine Learning in Blender

Artificial intelligence (AI) and machine learning (ML) are transforming various industries, and the world of 3D graphics is no exception. Blender, as a versatile and community-driven software, is embracing the potential of AI and ML to enhance its capabilities. In this section, we'll delve into the role of AI and machine learning in Blender and how these technologies are shaping the future of 3D graphics.

1. Character Animation and Rigging

AI-driven tools are simplifying the process of character animation and rigging in Blender. Machine learning algorithms can analyze and predict movement patterns, making it easier to create natural and realistic animations. Tools like auto-rigging and motion capture enhancement are becoming more accessible, saving artists time and effort.

```
# Example Python code for using an AI-driven auto-rigging tool in Blender

import bpy

# Select the character mesh

bpy.data.objects['Character'].select_set(True)

# Use the AI-driven auto-rigging tool

bpy.ops.rigging.auto_rig()
```

2. Procedural Content Generation

AI and ML algorithms are being employed to generate procedural content, including textures, landscapes, and environments. Blender's node-based shader editor and Python scripting capabilities allow artists to integrate AI-generated content seamlessly into their projects, resulting in dynamic and diverse scenes.

3. Denoising and Rendering

Rendering in Blender can be time-consuming, especially for complex scenes. AI-powered denoising techniques, such as NVIDIA's OptiX AI denoiser, are integrated into Blender's Cycles renderer. These denoising algorithms significantly reduce render times while maintaining image quality.

```
# Example Python code for enabling AI denoising in Blender's Cycles renderer

import bpy

# Access the Cycles render settings

cycles_settings = bpy.context.scene.cycles

# Enable AI denoising

cycles_settings.use_denoising = True

cycles_settings.denoiser = 'OPTIX'
```

4. Enhanced Procedural Texturing

AI is being used to generate realistic and high-resolution textures. Artists can leverage AI-generated textures to add intricate details to their 3D models. Blender's support for procedural texturing and node-based workflows allows seamless integration of AI-generated textures.

5. Artistic Assistance

AI-based tools can assist artists by generating ideas, suggesting design elements, and automating repetitive tasks. For instance, AI can recommend color palettes, lighting setups, or camera angles based on the desired artistic style or mood.

6. Physics Simulation

Machine learning techniques are improving the accuracy of physics simulations in Blender. AI-driven simulations can predict dynamic interactions between objects, resulting in more realistic and dynamic simulations for effects like cloth, fluids, and particles.

```
# Example Python code for utilizing AI-enhanced physics simulation in Blender

import bpy

# Access the physics settings

physics_settings = bpy.context.scene.physics

# Enable AI-enhanced fluid simulation

physics_settings.use_ai_fluid_simulation = True
```

7. Content Generation for AR and VR

Blender is adapting to the demands of augmented reality (AR) and virtual reality (VR) content creation. AI-driven tools can optimize 3D assets for real-time rendering, ensuring smooth experiences in AR and VR applications.

8. Educational Tools

AI and ML are being used to create educational tools within Blender. These tools can provide guided tutorials, suggest learning paths, and offer real-time feedback to help users improve their 3D skills.

The integration of AI and machine learning into Blender is driven by the desire to enhance creative workflows, reduce tedious tasks, and make 3D graphics more accessible to a broader audience. Blender's open-source nature and active community participation contribute to the rapid development and adoption of AI-driven features. As AI and ML technologies continue to advance, Blender is well-positioned to remain a cutting-edge tool for 3D artists and developers.

20.3 Blender in Emerging Technologies and Industries

Blender's versatility and open-source nature have led to its adoption in various emerging technologies and industries. In this section, we'll explore how Blender is making an impact in these fields, showcasing its adaptability and potential for innovation.

1. Virtual Reality (VR) and Augmented Reality (AR)

Blender plays a vital role in creating 3D content for VR and AR applications. VR experiences require immersive 3D environments, while AR apps need 3D assets that can interact with the real world. Blender's support for real-time rendering, 3D modeling, and animation makes it an ideal choice for content creation in these emerging technologies.

2. Architectural Visualization

Architects and designers increasingly use Blender for architectural visualization. Its ability to create realistic 3D models of buildings and interiors, coupled with advanced rendering capabilities, allows professionals to present their designs effectively. Blender's support for real-time rendering engines like Eevee is particularly valuable in this context.

```
# Example Python code for importing architectural models into Blender

import bpy
```

```
# Import an architectural model in a common format (e.g., FBX)

bpy.ops.import_scene.fbx(filepath='/path/to/
architectural_model.fbx')
```

3. Game Development

Blender has a growing presence in the game development industry. Game developers use it for asset creation, character modeling, level design, and animation. Blender's compatibility with popular game engines like Unity and Unreal Engine simplifies the integration of assets into game projects.

4. Medical Visualization and Simulation

In the medical field, Blender is used for visualizing complex medical data, creating anatomical models, and simulating medical procedures. Surgeons and educators benefit from Blender's capabilities in developing interactive medical training tools and educational content.

5. Education and Training

Blender's accessibility and open-source nature make it a valuable tool in educational settings. It is used to teach 3D modeling, animation, and digital art in schools and universities. Additionally, online tutorials and courses leverage Blender to provide hands-on learning experiences.

6. Film and Animation

Blender continues to make its mark in the film and animation industries. Independent filmmakers and animation studios use Blender for creating short films, TV series, and feature-length animations. Its comprehensive set of tools, including compositing and video editing, contributes to its growing popularity.

7. Product Design and Visualization

Product designers and manufacturers employ Blender for creating 3D prototypes, product visualizations, and marketing materials. Blender's ability to render photorealistic product images and animations is valuable for showcasing products before production.

8. Scientific Visualization

Scientists and researchers turn to Blender for scientific visualization, data representation, and simulations. It aids in visualizing complex scientific concepts and data, making it accessible to a wider audience.

9. Art and Entertainment

Blender's impact in the art and entertainment sectors extends beyond animation and film. Artists use Blender for digital art creation, sculpting, and motion graphics. The software's flexibility and extensive community support foster artistic exploration.

Blender's adaptability to various industries and technologies is a testament to its relevance in the ever-evolving landscape of 3D graphics and visualization. As emerging technologies continue to shape our world, Blender remains a versatile and accessible tool for creators, professionals, and innovators across diverse fields. Its open-source nature encourages collaboration and development, ensuring its continued growth and impact in emerging sectors.

20.4 Educating the Next Generation of Blender Artists

As Blender continues to evolve and gain prominence in various industries, it also plays a significant role in educating the next generation of 3D artists, designers, and developers. Blender's accessibility, community support, and comprehensive feature set make it an excellent tool for teaching and learning 3D graphics. In this section, we'll explore how Blender contributes to education and training in the field of computer graphics.

1. Incorporating Blender into Curricula

Educational institutions, from primary schools to universities, recognize the value of Blender as a teaching tool. Blender is integrated into curricula to teach 3D modeling, animation, rendering, and compositing. Students gain hands-on experience with industry-standard software while developing valuable skills for creative and technical careers.

2. Online Learning Resources

The Blender community actively contributes to educational initiatives by creating a wealth of online learning resources. Websites, forums, YouTube channels, and online courses offer tutorials, guides, and tips for Blender users of all skill levels. These resources provide self-paced learning opportunities, making it easier for aspiring artists to acquire Blender proficiency.

3. Blender Foundation's Education Program

The Blender Foundation, the organization behind Blender's development, supports educational initiatives through its Education Program. This program provides educators and institutions with resources, curriculum guidelines, and collaboration opportunities. It helps standardize Blender education and encourages the development of educational content.

4. Open Source and Cost-Effective

Blender's open-source nature eliminates the cost barrier for educational institutions. Schools and students can access Blender for free, reducing the financial burden associated with proprietary software licenses. This accessibility fosters a more inclusive and diverse learning environment.

5. Industry-Relevant Skills

Blender's feature set aligns with industry standards, ensuring that students acquire skills that are directly applicable to careers in animation, game development, visual effects, and more. Learning Blender prepares students for a wide range of creative and technical roles.

```
# Example Python code for a basic animation in Blender

import bpy

# Create a cube object

bpy.ops.mesh.primitive_cube_add(size=2)

# Set keyframes for animation

cube = bpy.context.object

cube.location.x = -5

cube.keyframe_insert(data_path="location", frame=1)

cube.location.x = 5
```

```
cube.keyframe_insert(data_path="location", frame=50)

# Play the animation

bpy.ops.screen.animation_play()
```

6. Artistic Expression and Creativity

Blender encourages artistic expression and creativity. Students can explore various aspects of digital art, from character design and sculpting to motion graphics and compositing. Blender's diverse community and open-ended workflows inspire students to develop their unique styles and projects.

7. Career Opportunities

Proficiency in Blender opens doors to diverse career opportunities. Graduates with Blender skills can pursue careers in animation studios, game development companies, architectural firms, advertising agencies, and more. Blender's versatility allows students to specialize in their areas of interest.

8. Blender Competitions and Challenges

The Blender community organizes competitions and challenges that provide students with opportunities to showcase their skills and creativity. These events foster healthy competition and offer exposure to industry professionals.

Educating the next generation of Blender artists not only empowers individuals with valuable skills but also contributes to the growth and sustainability of the Blender community. As Blender continues to advance and adapt to emerging trends, it remains a valuable tool for educators and students alike, nurturing a new generation of talented 3D artists and professionals.

20.5 Envisioning the Future of Blender and 3D Artistry

The future of Blender and 3D artistry is filled with exciting possibilities and innovations. As technology advances and creative boundaries continue to expand, Blender stands as a dynamic and adaptable tool at the forefront of this evolution. In this final section, we'll explore some key aspects of what the future might hold for Blender and the broader world of 3D graphics.

1. Realism and Immersion

Blender's rendering capabilities are expected to continue advancing, pushing the boundaries of realism in 3D graphics. As hardware improves and real-time rendering technologies become more sophisticated, artists will have the power to create truly immersive and lifelike experiences in fields like gaming, virtual reality, and architectural visualization.

2. AI-Powered Creativity

Artificial intelligence and machine learning will play an even more significant role in the creative process. AI-driven tools will assist artists in generating content, optimizing workflows, and automating repetitive tasks. Blender is likely to integrate more AI-powered features, making it easier for artists to bring their visions to life.

3. Accessibility and Inclusivity

Blender's commitment to being open source and free to use will continue to make it a standout choice for creators of all backgrounds. Its user-friendly interface and accessibility features will evolve to ensure that 3D graphics and artistry are accessible to individuals with diverse abilities.

4. Collaboration and Community

Blender's strong sense of community will remain a driving force behind its development. Artists, developers, and educators will continue to collaborate, share knowledge, and contribute to Blender's growth. The Blender Foundation's efforts to forge partnerships and foster collaboration will result in exciting projects and innovations.

5. Blender for Emerging Technologies

Blender will adapt to emerging technologies, including augmented reality (AR), virtual reality (VR), and mixed reality (MR). It will be a pivotal tool for creating 3D content that seamlessly integrates with these immersive experiences. The ability to design and visualize AR/VR worlds within Blender will become more prevalent.

6. Cross-Platform Integration

Blender's compatibility with other software tools and platforms will improve. Integration with industry-standard software, game engines, and online collaboration platforms will be streamlined, making it easier for professionals to work seamlessly within various pipelines.

```
# Example Python code for exporting Blender models to a popular game engine

import bpy

# Select the objects to export

bpy.ops.object.select_all(action='DESELECT')

bpy.context.view_layer.objects.active = None

bpy.data.objects['MyModel'].select_set(True)
```

```
# Export to a game engine format (e.g., Unity)

bpy.ops.export_scene.fbx(filepath='/path/to/exported/model.fbx', use_selection=True)
```

7. Blender's Role in Education

Blender's role in education will expand further. It will be integrated into more curricula and online courses, providing students with opportunities to learn and practice 3D graphics skills. The Blender Foundation's educational initiatives will continue to support educators and learners.

8. Environmental and Sustainability Initiatives

The Blender community's commitment to environmental sustainability will grow stronger. Efforts to reduce the carbon footprint of 3D graphics rendering and promote eco-friendly practices will become more prominent.

9. Artistic Freedom and Innovation

Blender will remain a haven for artistic freedom and innovation. Artists will explore new frontiers in digital artistry, pushing the boundaries of what's possible. Blender's open-ended workflows will empower artists to experiment, collaborate, and create groundbreaking work.

The future of Blender and 3D artistry is shaped by the collaborative spirit of its community, the rapid advancements in technology, and the boundless creativity of artists. As Blender continues to evolve, it remains a symbol of accessibility, inclusivity, and limitless artistic potential, ready to embrace the challenges and opportunities of the future.

www.ingramcontent.com/pod-product-compliance
Lightning Source LLC
LaVergne TN
LVHW090305210926
848480LV00001B/142